Visit: MelissaJanuary.com

MIC logo are registered Trademark of

MEKEI International Coaching

ISBN- 13: 978-1533500687

ISBN- 10: 1533500681

About the Founder

Melissa January is a public speaker, innovator, and community icon. A German native now residing in Suwanee, GA, 33-year-old Melissa has begun to create a legacy for herself that inspires and empowers all those who come into contact with her. Her drive to help others achieve more in life and realize the beauty and power that they possess was birthed via her own awakening. As an abuse survivor, Melissa knows firsthand what it's like to feel helpless and incomplete. "I've gone from pretending to be brave to being truly brave by being honest and living the life I always dreamed of having," states Melissa. It is now her goal to empower others so that they may develop greater self-esteem, higher expectations for themselves, and a refined sense of self-love.

Inspired to use her testimony to encourage others to aim higher, realize their purpose, and know their worth, Melissa decided to become certified as a licensed life coach. Successfully completing the certification process and receiving her licensure from the International Coaching Science Research Foundation, Melissa was ready to impact the world. In March of 2015 she moved forward with founding

MEKEI International Coaching, a company designed to help people awaken to the multitude of possibilities that are present in life. Per the company's slogan, MEKEI is dedicated to "Creating positive change and achieving extraordinary results". As a certified international life coach and motivational speaker, Melissa has addressed several organizations, prominent businesses, and private groups regarding topics ranging from personal growth, domestic violence, and motivating our youth.

Melissa's coaching style is attributed to her natural enthusiasm, endearing personality, and incredible sense of compassion. Additionally, her background and life experiences have helped to shape her understanding of life and the importance of being the best individual you can be by loving yourself and aspiring for greatness. Her sense of humor blended with her unbiased honesty is ultimately what connects her to her clients and enables her to push them to reach for their dreams. Melissa's commitment to her coaching endeavors is both sincere and purposeful. With each client she assists, she aims to see them through not only their victories, of which she prays each client experiences many, but she is also dedicated to seeing them through even the rough patches in life. Melissa fosters a personable coaching relationship that aids in the success of each client's outcome. For her, the client's success and wellbeing is the driving force for her company.

With her life coaching initiative in place, Melissa took her dedication to uplifting others a step further by focusing on today's youth. In the later part of March 2015, she founded #GurlsOnTheMove, a mentoring group for female youth. Operating under the motto, "be the motivation you wish to inspire," #GurlsOnTheMove is dedicated to encouraging young women to pursue their dreams. Meeting with the girls as a group or even on an individual basis once a month, Melissa and her team focuses on that which interests the young ladies and expounds upon how they can cultivate their interests and dreams into a lucrative, positive, and beneficial reality. From boosting self-esteem, to overcoming societal hardships, to working on aspirations within various industries, #GurlsOnTheMove is all about empowerment, forward thinking, and positivity.

Having an extensive resume in support of her coaching and public speaking endeavors, Melissa is well on her way to being a self-help expert. Fondly referred to as the 'Challenge Guru', Melissa remains humble and true to her original mission and desire to simply empower others to be the best them possible. Her efforts to do so haven't gone unnoticed. In April of 2015, Melissa was inducted into the National Association of Professional Women. Within this professional affiliation, Melissa has been able to expand her brand while also fine-tuning her own expertise.

Melissa realizes how important it is for everyone to know their worth and live up to their full potential. She also realizes that not everyone can afford a coaching service to help them improve upon various areas of their lives. For this reason, in the next couple of years Melissa aspires to create a nonprofit coaching outreach company that is supported by major organizations within the United States. The primary focus of this initiative would be to provide a platform where each business and each individual from various backgrounds and walks of life can actually learn from one another, therefore empowering each other nationwide.

Always thinking of ways to improve herself and to improve the way that she helps others, Melissa has dedicated her life to giving back to the world by empowering individuals one at time. Her ideas, methods, and endeavors are backed by her passion and conviction in the power of positive thinking. In the years to come, she hopes that the legacy she's begun to piece together will materialize in a fashion that motivates others to follow their dreams and love themselves enough to know that they too deserve more out of life.

Dedication

**Special dedication to my brother who tragically passed away on December, 20th 2012,

Born May 10, 1978 – Deceased December 20, 2012.

We shared lots of years, and a whole lot of fun, but God has called you home to his son.

I just can't believe it has ended this way there were so many things I had to say…

it's too late for that now, it will just have to wait, until the day that I see you at the heavenly gate.
May your soul rest well, my beloved brother, but the day is not over, because we shall share another

your tragic death has left a big whole, but I'll try not to fret you're now, a free soul.

So when times are great, and happy as such, I'll think of you MY Brother. I miss you so much.

Dein Schwesterherz, Melissa January!

The adventures of my life weren't always fun. I fought through hard times and found myself fighting a battle that seemed as though I could not win. I led myself on a journey to find myself and learned that life is what you make out of it. It was a struggle going from life to death and death to life. At times, I was ready to give up. This Book is dedicated to all women. My hope is to empower you and fill your heart with a new spirit regarding how to deal with your life after being mentally and physically abused.

Booking Inquiries:

M.January85@Gmail.com

FB: Melissa January
IG: iam_melissajanuary
Twitter: @Melissa_January

~ Acknowledgements~

Wow, I cannot believe the time has finally come for this dream to be real. I never set out to become a writer but I thank God for steering me in that direction. I thank God for bringing people and situations into my life at the right time because their timing has meant everything!

Thank you to my Mom, for always being there and for being you. Thank you so much! I Love you!

Thanks to my son. He loves to see his mommy pursuing her dreams. His words are always so genuine. "Mom you know you can do it!" Got to love him.

Thanks to my sisters. You are truly what family is about. Love you! Thanks for all you have done!!!

Thanks to my other half for always supporting me, letting me run ideas past you, and for helping me make decisions. Thanks for encouraging me to pursue my writing passion and for always having my back 100%. Love you!

To all my family, friends, and colleagues who were waiting for the day this book would come out: It's here and it's time to rack up copies of it. Pass it on!

I would like to give special thanks to Dr. Carlton N. Young for inspiring me.

It has taken a village to get this into the hands of my readers and I am grateful to each and every one of you.

Sincerely,

Melissa January

~ Table of Contents~

~ Chapter 1~

Romance

"When someone shows you who they are, believe them."

"Good afternoon, sir. ID and registration please!"

The gentleman in the vehicle was nodding his head to the music, paying me no attention. His music was blasting so loud that I could barely hear my own voice as I issued the standard request. Feeling my patience thinning, I pursed my lips into a patronizing grin and politely asked again.

"Sir, your ID and registration please. And could you please turn the volume down?"

Gradually he turned down the music while handing me his documents. I confirmed the validity of his license and the status of his vehicle's registration before finally sending him on his way. "Thank you. Have a great day, sir."

With a massive grin on his face he turned the music back up and sped off. *What a jerk,* I thought to myself.

The afternoon shift was exhausting at times and customers like him were not making my day any easier. But, I had to make the best out of it since I'd decided to make money first and pursue my education later. This job was a means to an end and I had to keep reminding myself of that to avoid becoming discouraged and quit prematurely. The plan was to work there for a little while or at least until I figured out what I was really going to do with my life. My choices were either going to school for nursing or becoming a Culinary Arts professor. Ultimately, I decided to register at the BOS Kitzingen (Upper Vocational School).

Working security for Securitas was not my ideal job, but the pay was great and the daily duties were pretty simple. Like I said, it was merely a means to an end. One of the drawbacks of being assigned to the security gate for military personnel in Kitzingen was the myriads of guys that called themselves flirting with me on a daily basis. Their come-ons and pickup lines were tired and effortless as if it wasn't enough of a turn off that they chose to harass me while doing a thankless job. Never once had I given any of the men passing through any consideration. They were just faces in a sea of many that I had to communicate with for the duration of each of my shifts.

As my shift came closer to its end, I began to cheer up because it was girls' night out. Every once in a while me and some of my girls would get together for a night of fun. We would choose between dinner, movies or clubbing. Whatever we did, we had a good time letting our hair down and relaxing away the long, stressful week we'd all just endured. This week, it only felt right to dance (and drink) away our trying work week at the club. We decided upon B&S, our favorite spot. It was one of the most well-known spots on a Friday night. People would travel from afar just to get their party on because of its potent cocktails, loud urban music, large dance floor and unbeatable specials. The party at B&S actually starts outside in the parking lot. No one ever had a problem standing in the long line waiting to be admitted because the sound of the music floated its way outside of the large front double doors into the parking lot. Those in line moved to the beat while mingling with their crew and others around them—all waiting to experience the live entertainment inside.

My crew were such regulars that the bartender would often have a round of our favorite drink ready for us as soon as we walked in the building. The Famous Master Blaster was a mix of Red Bull, Champagne, and Vodka. If you consumed two of them in one night, it was surely a wrap for you. Tonight was no different. As the four of us, Mindy, Bianca, Jessica, and myself, approached the bar, the bartender already had four glasses situated in front of the four barstools directly in the center of the bar.

"Evening ladies," he greeted us as he poured up the potent blend for each of us.

"Hey Rodney!" we sang in unison, each ready for the first sip of the cocktail that we knew would put us in an ultra-relaxed head space.

Rodney had seen us as we'd entered the door and wasted no time in getting up our order. The drink was smooth and just as perfect as usual. He watched us as we all savored the flavor, nodding our heads in complete satisfaction. Content with the knowledge that we were happy, Rodney nodded in return and moved on to wait on the next group of party-goers strolling through the entrance.

We finished our first round and had begun to get our groove on the dance floor when this tall muscular man started to head in my direction. I saw him from my peripheral, not knowing what to expect and assuming that he was actually trying to get to someone else, I moved slightly to the right to allow him to pass me. The abrupt halt in his gait stunned me and I looked up as he reached his hands out towards me expectantly.

"Care to dance with me?" I heard him ask over the bass of the music.

I was caught off guard and didn't know what to say. I wasn't a virgin to men coming on to me, but the immediate arousal he sparked had me puzzled and speechless.

He asked me again. "Can I get a dance with you, beautiful?" Even over the beat of the music, his voice was like a slice of heaven—a strong baritone with an air of confidence and conviction.

My friends had long since looked up to witness the encounter. As their bodies continued to sway to the music their eyes were glued on me while trying to stifle their giggles. They whispered loudly to one another wondering if I would accept his offer to dance or simply blow him off like I was used to doing. Only this time, my hesitation didn't reveal my decision clearly to anyone, myself included.

I looked down at his strong, large hands and swallowed hard before looking back up into his dark, penetrating eyes. "I'm sorry," I said, shooting him down. The current song ended and my voice returned to a normal octave. "Me and my girls are chilling tonight." I shrugged. "Ladies night," I offered a brief explanation before turning around and rejoining my group just as the next set began.

I noticed that he continued to stand there for a minute as if he was anticipating me changing my mind. The girls and I huddled close together dancing and laughing at the situation but I couldn't help but glance back in his direction. My movements slowed down taking me offbeat as recognition slapped me in the face. *Oh my goodness*, I thought. *That's the same guy from earlier today. The same guy who came into the gate blasting his music so loud that I could not hear my own words.* I wondered if he recognized me outside of my uniform. Immediately I turned my back to him, not giving him the satisfaction of assuming that I was reconsidering his offer. *No, you definitely won't be getting a chance with me*, I thought as I tried to refocus my attention on enjoying the night with my girls.

Halfway into the next song, he took me by surprise by trying yet again. The feel of his hand on my arm sent shivers up my spine and I jumped as I jerked my head to the side to see who had dared to touch me.

"Come on, Ma," he said, leaning towards me so that I could hear him over the music. "At least tell me your name. Talk to me please," he pleaded, never letting go of my arm.

I shook my head, standing firm in my decision. "No, sir. I'm here with my girls and we're just trying to have a good time. Now please excuse me."

I stared him straight in the eyes searching for any hint of recognition but seeing none. I knew that there was a significant difference between my day and night appearance. It was feasible that how I looked wearing my uniform and how I looked in the shape hugging, black tube dress that I was wearing appeared to him to be two completely different women. Still, I'd assumed that he would recognize the sternness in my face and the way my eyes pierced through his with a seriousness as my lips pursed together in disdain, just like earlier in the day. It was clear that he didn't remember the girl he'd given nothing but attitude to a little earlier. It was not unusual that guys show you little to no respect as a female security officer. It was a sad truth, but it was validated by the fact that this man didn't even recognize the person standing before him.

Disgusted and done with repeatedly denying this douche bag, I walked off the dance floor in pursuit of a second drink. Not one to back down from a challenge, he followed me to the bar.

"Dude, what are you some kind of stalker?" I huffed, turning around to face him as I waited for Rodney to bring me another Master Blaster.

With a huge smile on his face as if I hadn't just dissed him twice on the dance floor, he said, "Hey, gorgeous. My name is J. I was born in Puerto Rico and raised in Louisiana and I am 27 years old."

The way he rattled off his background information like he was applying for a job, I couldn't help but to laugh. "Okay, really? That's how you going to make it work for yourself now?"

He continued on despite my fit of giggles. "I have a daughter; she is three years old."

I held up my right hand and cradled my stomach with my left hand. "Okay, Stop! Stop, Stop, Stop! That's enough!" I had to make him stop before he stood there and recapped his entire life story.

Rodney brought me my drink and I sipped it gingerly as I recomposed myself and took a good look at J. Instead of 27 he looked more like 37. I shook my head feeling vindicated in my original assessment of him earlier in the day—asshole.

"Look, it's really nice to meet you J, but I don't believe anything that you just said," I told him honestly. I figured he'd had far too much to drink to actually think that his lines were going to get him some play. "Let's continue this conversation a little later, okay. You might want to chill with some water if you seriously want to talk to me." I moved to walk away.

J sidestepped me, blocking my exit from our failed conversation. "I'm dead serious," he said solemnly. "Everything I am telling you is the truth, Ma. But okay. I'll get at you later."

I walked away from him and headed to the dance floor with my drink still in hand just as the DJ started to play the slow jams. That was my cue. It was definitely time to go. But, as I scoped the perimeter of the dance floor I noticed that each of my girls were booed up and dancing with somebody. "Ugh!" I exclaimed, realizing that I was the odd one out. Reluctantly, I headed back over to the bar where J was still standing. It was apparent in that moment that I was not going to be able to shake this dude, at least until the DJ reverted back to playing up-tempo jams. For the moment I had nothing else to do but entertain J the liar and nurse my drink.

"So, are you ready to tell me some real things about you?" I asked, taking a seat on the stool next to where he stood tall.

"I didn't lie about anything to start with, gorgeous," he insisted. "If you would just please give me a chance to get to know you before trying to sum a brother up. That's all I'm asking…for now."

His cockiness wasn't lost on me with his last words. "We'll see," I replied before settling in for what I assumed would be a highly fabricated conversation.

By the end of the night we finally exchanged numbers. Although I was a tad skeptical at first, I had to admit that J had drawn me in during the course of the evening. There was something wildly dominant and rugged about him, yet attentive and charming.

As I stuck my key into my front door during the wee hours of the morning, I felt my phone vibrating inside of my clutch bag. Wondering if maybe it was one of the girls in need of help or something, I fished my phone out and answered quickly. "Hello?"

"Did you make it home safely, gorgeous?" It was J.

My heart fluttered at the sound of his voice blaring in my ear. I could hear the slur in his words but the sentiment behind his call was touching nonetheless. “Yeah,” I replied, turning the key in the lock opening my front door. “I just got here.”

“Good. I’d hate for anyone to come along and kidnap an angel. That wouldn’t be right.”

I closed and locked the door while giggling to his drunken compliments. “Shouldn’t you be getting in the bed?”

“How can I sleep when my mind is filled with images of your beauty?”

“You’re so full of it,” I responded, heading to my bedroom to prepare myself for bed.

“No, no, no. I am not worthy to behold such a beautiful sight. I just needed to talk to you one more time…hear your beautiful voice one more time…” His words began to trail off as I changed into a t-shirt and slipped between the covers of my bed.

“Go to bed,” I said, yawning.

“Can I ask you a question?”

I closed my eyes as a cradled the phone under my chin with the assistance of my pillows. “Mmmhmm.”

“Did it hurt?”

“Did what hurt?” I asked sheepishly.

“When you fell from heaven.”

I giggled naively, drunk with alcohol and the euphoria that J created with his constant attempts to verbally woe me. My thoughts fluttered into fragments and then into silence as I was lured to sleep by sounds of him declaring his attraction to me.

~ Chapter 2~

Truth or Dare

"Let's play truth or dare
or just dare because
nobody tells the truth anymore."

The next morning, I woke up to a text message from J that made my heart flutter.

Good morning, Gorgeous. I hope you didn't drool all over your phone and hopefully we are able to continue our phone conversation later. Have a great day!

I beamed from ear to ear thinking it was so cute that he would think to hit me up before starting his day. I racked my brain trying to remember what it was that we'd mumbled about in the wee hours of the morning in our drunken slumber. I recalled him telling me that he was originally from Louisiana and that he'd just returned from war. His unit was one of the first to be shipped out to Iraq. I also remembered him saying that he used to be a professional football player and that he got hurt in the first month of his career. After that incident he was not able to continue his football career so he became a soldier. He'd dropped out of college to go pro and felt that the military was a good thing to fall back on since he didn't have a degree.

As I re-read his good morning text, I decided to send a cordial one of my own.

Good morning, sir! Wishing you an awesome day as well.

It didn't take long for his reply to come back.

It will only be awesome if you agree to have dinner with me tonight.

I grinned from ear to ear at his assertiveness.

I believe we can make that happen.

After giving him my address and setting a time for our date later I went about doing my normal Saturday morning routine. The difference between this Saturday and all the ones before it was that there was a little extra joy in my movement. The anticipation of seeing him later had me energized and cheerful. I didn't know what it was, but the mere thought of J kept me smiling.

***

We decided upon a steak house that was near my home. The ambiance was nice—not too crowded, low lighting, soft music playing, and candles lit on every table. We ordered our food and settled into our first real, post bar, conversation. I found myself looking into his eyes intently as he spoke, trying to get a true feel for him as a person. The more I looked, the more mesmerized I became with his overall physique and the way he seemed to just command attention. He was a confident man and I liked that.

"So, you said that you went to college before going pro," I stated, taking a sip of my lemonade. "What college did you go to?"

"Mississippi State University," he answered.

"What were you studying?"

"Early childhood education. I wanted to be a teacher. You know, do something good in the community and help kids live up to their full potential."

I smiled. "That's commendable."

"Yeah, but my passion for football was so extreme and everyone knew I was meant to play in the pros. When the draft came around my sophomore year of college I felt like I needed to go for it. I had the highest ranking stats of any freshman in the south my first year playing for A&M so…I went for it."

"Nothing like living out your dreams."

He nodded. "Exactly. It's like, when there's something I want there's nothing at all that can stop me from getting it." He paused and looked at me meaningfully. "I never settle for less than what I feel I deserve."

I looked into his eyes and remembered the way he'd been so persistent the night before at B&S. *At least he's honest about his tenacity*, I thought. "And you felt you deserved a spot on one of the pro teams?"

"You know it! When the Lions picked me up you couldn't tell me nothing. It was probably one of the proudest days of my life." He lowered his head to look down at the steak that our waiter had just walked over and placed before him. "But, the day that I tore my ACL was the most traumatic experience ever," he said in a somber tone. “All my hopes for a better life, my dreams…everything kinda ripped apart the moment I felt that rip in the leg. It was hard to accept that I wasn’t going to be able to have the career and the life that I’d envisioned for myself.”

I cut up my steak and continued listening to him discuss his feelings about his past. I wanted him to know that I was genuinely interested in his story so I didn’t interrupt and I made sure to keep our eye contact going as I ate.

“When the doctor confirmed that I wouldn’t be able to play anymore I had to hurry up and cope with the reality and then decide what I was going to do with my life,” he said.

“And going back to school to finish your degree wasn’t an option?” I asked.

His eyebrow rose but quickly fell as he responded. “Once you’ve really been out on your own and start seeing a little change it’s hard to go back to a life of taking out loans, living on campus, or depending on your parents. I needed to do something to keep me self-sufficient…something that was going to get me at least some of the income that I was prepared to receive as a ball player."

"And the military provided you with that?"

"The military provided me with that and more. Not only was I able to jump right into a lucrative career but school cost-free became an option, I was able to travel and meet people from all over the globe and different walks of life…my sergeants taught me a lot and the entire experience made me a more disciplined man."

I smiled at the thought. "Nothing wrong with that."

J smiled back and took a bite of his steak.

"So, what was it like in Iraq?" I asked nonchalantly as I forked some of my baked potato into my mouth.

He shrugged and shook his head. "Sandy, gritty, hot, and loud." That was all he offered by way of a response.

"I'm sure it was a pretty surreal experience," I prodded. "I mean; I still don't even understand the logic in sending our troops over to another country to—"

"It's not exactly a part of my career or memories that I like to revisit," he interjected firmly. His eyes were bold and dead set on mine.

I nodded my understanding. There was no telling what he'd seen or endured while overseas and the last thing I wanted to do was re-traumatize him by asking questions and forcing him to recap the ordeal. I let it go and we went on to talk about less depressing things until our meals were finished and we decided to move on to a nearby bar.

The bar was nearly empty for a Saturday night. In the scarcity of the crowd I recognized one of my girlfriends off in the cut. I waved at her as J and I walked through the maze of tables.

"What's up, J?" a female's voice boomed out behind us as we passed a table.

I turned around to see who had spoken and locked eyes with a petite chick rocking long Cleopatra type of braids. She smirked at me but I simply turned around and looked over at J. He acted as if he hadn't heard the girl at all.

"Melissa!!!" My friend, Mia, was calling me over to her table.

I looked at J to see if he minded stopping to say hello and he nodded in Mia's direction. Together we approached the table and J stood back as Mia and I embraced.

"Hey, girl!" Mia gushed. "Where you coming from? I haven't seen you--" Her voice trailed off as she looked over my shoulder and finally took a good look at the handsome man that was escorting me. "J? Hey! I didn't know you were back!"

I was astonished as I looked from Mia to J. "You two know each other? Like, really?"

"Girl, who doesn't know J?" Mia joked before giving J a quick hug and returning her attention to her watered down drink.

Seems like he's a little more popular than he's telling me, I thought to myself as I stood there feeling foolish, wondering how many other women in the scantily populated bar knew J in some form or fashion. "Well, it was good to see you again, girl," I told Mia, ready to abandon any conversation that she thought was about to pop off after that awkward moment. I allowed J to lead me over to the bar where I quickly took a seat on a high stool, anxious for a drink. At that moment I recalled that he'd told me over the phone that he'd only been back home now for six months since returning from Iraq. I wondered if his popularity had been established before or after his deployment. Judging from Mia's shock at his return I had to conclude that the former was true.

"You okay or do you want to leave?" he asked, taking in my skeptic expression and sudden quietness.

As much as I wanted to leave and remove myself from the pointed stares of the two women he was familiar with, I just shook my head. "No, I'm okay."

"You know this is a small city right?" he asked me as he waved over the bartender who was steadily chatting up a single bleached blond female.

"Mmmhmm."

"I've been to this bar like twice," he explained. "It's the kinda place were the patrons are regulars and everybody knows everybody."

The bartender approached and we ordered our cocktails. For me the date at this point was over. I was barely present mentally for the small banter we exchanged while sitting at the bar. By the time we walked out of the door I felt a sense of relief wash over me.

"Where to now?" he asked.

I smiled politely and made my request. "If you could just take me back home that's fine. I think I'm ready to call it a night."

He opened his mouth to say something and then stopped himself. Nodding his consent, he held the passenger door open for me as I climbed into his car and then walked over to get into the driver's seat. The ride home was quiet but my thoughts were loud. Once we pulled up to my house I didn't wait for him to open the door for me although he'd gotten out to do so. I stood in front of him and he smiled at me expectantly.

"I had a good time with you," he said.

Again, I gave him a polite smile. "So did I." It was true, up until he'd taken me to that bar.

He took a step towards me and leaned forward but I turned my head away. "No kiss?" he asked.

"No, sir," I informed him. I touched his arm gingerly. "Thank you for dinner. Good night." I stepped to the side and walked around him to ascend the walkway leading to my front door. I knew he was watching me as I let myself in so I waved goodbye just before shutting the door. I took a deep breath and kicked my heels off by the door before walking to my kitchen for a bottle of water.

I didn't know how to process the evening we'd just spent together. While I was engrossed in his charm and aura, I was a little weirded out by his popularity with the women in the bar, even one of my own associates. Before I could sort out my thoughts and feelings, my cell phone began to chime. Eagerly, I reached into my purse and pulled it out. Seeing his name on the CALLER ID made me raise a brow. "Hello?" I answered cautiously.

"Just checking to make sure you were inside safe and sound," he said. "Doors all locked and you're comfortable."

I laughed as I hurried to my front window to check the driveway. He was gone. "Dude, you just watched me walk into the house."

"Yes, but anything could have happened after you closed the door and I drove off. I just wanted to make sure that my angel was nice and safe."

I laughed at his corniness and all my misgivings from the bar seemed to fly right out of my front window. I couldn't stay mad at him. The truth is that I was a sucker for a gentleman and the way that he was so considerate and attentive to me made my insecurities seem so futile. On top of that, he was extremely fine. His great looks and that awesomely sculpted body made it even harder for me to not like him. I couldn't help it. J was quickly getting me hooked on the essence of him.

"What are you doing?" he asked me.

I moved away from my window and headed back to the kitchen. “Getting some water before settling down to watch some TV or something.”

“I love your German accent,” he told me. “It just makes me want to come through the phone and kiss the lips your words are flowing from.”

I giggled. I wanted to tell him that I loved his American drawl but I couldn’t get out the words.”

“What are you plans for tomorrow?”

“Resting,” I told him. “Before getting prepared for another busy week. You?”

“The same. Definitely gotta be in front of my TV for the game tomorrow afternoon?”

I grabbed my bottle of water and returned to the living room where I sank down onto my sofa and clicked on the television. “Oh?”

“Yeah, my team is playing. It’s agony to watch the game knowing that if circumstances had been different I’d actually be playing in it.”

"Hmmm, I can imagine how that would be frustrating," I said. *Why torture yourself like that*, I thought but decided to keep the question to myself.

"Man, when I look at the way these boys run these plays these days I just wanna scream. Nobody was getting more passes in rushing than me, but this dude they got now…his speed ain't 'bout nothing."

As he continued to talk about the current lineup for the Lions and his days playing with the team, I found myself saying a bunch of 'oh, okay's' and 'uh-huh' whenever I deemed it necessary. I didn't know much about football or any sport for that matter partly because I wasn't from the states and partly because I was just never exposed to any of it. Since I had no clue what he was talking about I couldn't really offer any intelligent responses so I just allowed him to lead and carry the conversation. That seemed to work out just fine for J because he talked for nearly an hour about his glory days with just as much as excitement as a kid at Christmas. It became apparent to me that although he no longer played, football was still a major part of his life.

After a while he grew quiet. The silence jolted me and prompted me to speak. “Hello?”

“I’m still here,” he stated before clearing his voice. “Umm…Melissa, may I ask you something?”

I changed the channel to Bravo and caught the middle of Americas Next Top Model rerun. “Sure,” I replied. “What is it?”

“Would you like to be my girlfriend?”

The question was so endearing and almost juvenile. It reminded me of an elementary school crush. But the sincerity of it was touching and I appreciated the way he seemed so sure of what he wanted yet so timid about coming out with it. I almost couldn’t believe my ears and questioned if maybe I’d just daydreamed it as he babbled on about the Lions. “Are you serious right now?” I asked him.

“I wanted to ask you face to face but I’m kinda shy about stuff like that.” He chuckled. “No dude wants to get shot down in person. At least by phone I can save face, you know?”

I was flattered and amused at the same time. “You’ve known me all of two days and you’re sure this is what you want?”

“I’m the kinda guy that doesn’t have to drag his feet on anything,” he replied. “I see what I want and I go for it.”

There he was again letting me know how much of a go-getter he was in every aspect of his life. I knew that if I didn’t say yes tonight he’d ask again soon and keep going until I finally gave in. But he didn’t have to go through those extremes this time. “Yes,” I said. “I think I’d like to be your girlfriend.” I felt really good. I was throwing caution to the wind and making a decision based on the euphoria this man created within me. *Why not*, I reasoned with myself. *He seems levelheaded, attentive, and entertaining*. The fact that he took it old school and asked me to be his girl verses us just falling into a routine and throwing a label on it later impressed me. I didn’t even know that guys still did that.

***

From the moment that I’d agreed to be J’s girlfriend he began to treat me like a queen. The flowers, gifts, dinners, and surprises were endless. I was pretty sure that I had what every woman dreamed of—a man that considered my needs, spoiled me rotten, made a decent living, and was extremely sexy. We spent nearly every day together and I never once had a complaint about anything. Three months into this blissful routine we'd adopted, he changed the game for me.

J decided to cook dinner at my house. Nothing too lavish, salmon with baked potatoes and asparagus. I loved the way he made everything romantic and on this night he remained true to form. He lit a candle in the middle of my dining room table and poured us up some glasses of pink champagne, which was my favorite. As I sat moved to sit down in the chair at the place setting he arranged for me, J grabbed me by my hands and looked into my eyes. I wasn't sure what was going on and for just a split second I was afraid that he was going to tell me that he was being deployed yet again.

"What?" I asked. "What is it?" The serious expression on his face had me nervous. "What's going on, J?"

"Before we have dinner and before the evening goes any further I need to ask you something."

"What?" I whispered, feeling a lump forming in my throat.

He caressed my hands with his as he spoke slowly. "This time with you has been amazing. I know a good thing when I see it, Melissa. Will you marry me?"

My body wavered and my head became light. Instantly my hands withdrew from his and I had to take a seat in my chair. As a sat I looked up at him while he continued to stand before me with his eyes piercing into mine awaiting my response. Speech was lost to me. I knew in my spirit that I'd long since fallen head over heels in love with J, but we'd only been together a short while. The rational side of me knew that it was irresponsible to accept his proposal knowing that we still had so much to learn about the other. But looking into his eyes and seeing the longing and expectancy there, I didn't know how to tell him that I didn't think we were ready for such a serious and final step.

"I've loved you from the moment I first saw you," he told him as if reading my mind and obviously sensing my hesitation.

My own thoughts traveled back to the actual first time that we'd met and I knew that the statement was a little untrue. He didn't even remember the rude encounter we'd had the day he'd come through my security checkpoint. But, I didn't dare correct him during this vulnerable moment.

"I know what I want, baby, and I want you," he said. "I knew the moment our eyes met Melissa, that I was going to make you my wife."

My heart ached but I had to be honest with him. I didn't want us to make a premature move only to resent it later. "I think…I-I-I think we should wait," I stuttered. "I think we should…we should get to know one another just a little bit better."

The sadness that spread across his face brought tears to my eyes. It pained me to tell him no when he'd apparently been so gung-ho about proposing then and there. I remembered his statement months ago about the shame of being shot down in person and immediately wanted to take back the words and kiss away the pain etched in his jaw line. I stood up and placed my arms around his neck and kissed his lips with more passion than I ever had before. He returned the gesture and we continued that way for several seconds. Pulling back, I looked up into his eyes. “I love you and I’m not saying no indefinitely,” I explained to him. “I’m just saying not right now.”

He kissed my nose softly. “I understand,” he said blankly before withdrawing from our embrace. “Come on, let’s eat before the food gets cold.”

And just like that we settled back into the groove of our night in. Although we chatted about other, unimportant things, my mind was still lingering on the fact that J wanted to marry me. I knew enough about him to know that this was something he was adamant about. Because of that, I knew he’d propose to me again. I just hoped that he did it at a time when I would feel comfortable saying yes.

***

It was a beautiful Saturday evening and we were driving through the city in his two door 3-series BMW. Our fingers were laced together as he navigated the roads and the wind whipped through my hair in a carefree manner. Life was good.

"Babe, do you think you need a new car?" he asked out of nowhere.

I turned to him and wrinkled my nose at the randomness. "No, my car's just fine, honey." *Of course I'd like a new car*, I thought. *But I'm not about to ask you to buy me one. Who does that?* We'd been dating for six months at this point and I didn't feel comfortable asking him to make such a large investment in me.

"Okay then," he said as if he was mulling through his thoughts. "Well, how about a vacation? Would you allow me to take you on a vacation?"

"A vacation," I repeated, considering the idea. I didn't want to turn it down but I felt a little awkward going on a vacation with someone I barely even knew. Before I could voice any of my concerns or have the opportunity to back out, J topped his offer.

"We can go wherever you want to go, baby," he said. "Anywhere in the world."

The possibilities were plentiful but I knew without hesitation exactly where I wanted to go. I wanted to go see my family in Atlanta, Georgia. I hadn't seen my sisters and nieces in years and now would be the perfect opportunity if he was serious.

"What's it gonna be, baby?" he asked.

"Atlanta," I said decidedly.

He turned to me with a shocked expression. "Atlanta? Out of all the places in the world you want to go to Atlanta, Georgia?"

"Mmmhmm." I pursed my lips together for a second before explaining my position and prayed that he would understand. "I have family there and I haven't seen any of them in ages. I figured it would be a good chance to get away and to reconnect. I know you were probably thinking of something more romantic..."

"Turn in your vacation time and let's make it happen," he said, cutting me off and squeezing my hand. "First class flight to Atlanta here we come."

"Really?" I squealed. I couldn't believe his generosity.

"Really. Whatever you want, never hesitate to ask. I got you."

I leaned over and kissed his cheek frantically over and over nearly causing him to swerve off of the road. "Oh my goodness! You're so amazing! Thank you, thank you, thank you!"

J smiled and continued driving with his posture poised and his head cocked to the side in a satisfied manner. I was on cloud nine.

***

True to his word, J got us first class tickets to Atlanta. We indulged in champagne during the flight and were picked up at the airport by a car service that he'd arranged early on. Because it was important for me to see my sisters immediately, we made that our first stop. The reunion was brief but I promised them that we'd have plenty of time to catch up during our stay. After leaving my family we headed to the mall. J led me around Lenox Mall shelling out cash for any and everything that I even looked like I wanted. At one point, he led me into a jewelry store and admitted that he was curious as to what type of engagement ring I would be interested in. The thought of getting married had seeped back into my mind and once again I felt my stomach knot up with nervousness. As I tried on ring after ring, I wondered when he was planning to propose again. Seeing the beautiful diamonds on my finger made me realize that the moment was probably a lot closer than I knew. But, surprisingly J didn't push me while we were in the store. He simply observed my reactions to each ring and when I grew tired of window shopping we moved on.

Our next stop was a hair salon. Since I could not decide what look I wanted to go for J huffed and told me he would just be back in a couple of hours. But, before he could exit the shop I told him I was just going to buy a wig.

"A wig?" he asked, standing at the exit.

I nodded. "Mmmhmm. It's an easy way to switch up my look," I said as I ran my hair through my unruly natural locks.

J gritted his teeth. He didn't like the idea of the wig. "Why can't you just get something done to your hair? We're on vacation. We're gonna be taking lots of pictures. Don't you want to look decent?"

I was slightly offended. “You don’t think I look decent just the way I am?”

“I’m saying…we’re going to be going out and stuff. I would think that you would want to do something different…something more tamed.”

“We’re on vacation,” I repeated him. “I’m in relax mode. I don’t wanna get my hair all straightened and have to worry about it getting messed up and stuff. It’ll be fine,” I assured him as I moved towards the register with the wig I’d chosen.

J exited the salon and waited for me in the car. I knew he was displeased with my decision but to me my hairstyle wasn’t such a big deal. I figured he’d get over it by the time we pulled out of the parking lot.

Later that night we went out. We left my sister Charlene's house at 7 PM. in an attempt to miss the downtown traffic. But, the highways were jammed nonetheless and then there was a huge line to get into the club that we were visiting. Around 9 PM we were finally standing inside of the club. My two sisters Charlene and Denise were with their husbands and my other sister from another mother, my old friend Victoria, was also there. We were all pretty hot and humid after standing in line for over an hour outside in the southern evening heat. I was thirsty and felt inclined to get myself a drink. As I was headed over to the bar, J followed right behind.

He grabbed my arm and whispered into my ear over the music. “Don’t leave my sight. This is not Germany, honey.”

I winced from his grasp. “Okay, I get it,” I replied feeling slightly annoyed.

Once at the bar I ordered a gin and juice. It wasn’t my customary drink so, I had no clue what made me ask for it. J ordered a Long Island Iced Tea and while we waited on the drinks I grabbed two mints from a nearby dish on the bar top. I popped the mints into my mouth and felt them instantly numb my taste buds. When my drink arrived it looked like a glass full of gin with just a splash of Orange Juice and lots of ice. But, as I started sipping it I felt the iciness going down my throat, cooling off my body. It felt so refreshing, like drinking a glass of ice cold juice. With my taste buds numbed and the liquor being so smooth, I forgot that I was actually drinking pure alcohol. I couldn't stop myself from guzzling the drink.

About five minutes later everyone else had their drinks in their hand and was ready to party. As I moved to stand up to accompany them to the dance floor I felt myself beginning to zone out. I couldn't see anything legibly; everything was a blur. I could hardly hear anything. All the noises around me seemed to blend into one hushed monotone wail. All I could manage to make out was a huge security guard who was standing in front of me.

"What's wrong with you?" he asked me in a frustrated tone. He'd been moving his mouth for a minute and I assumed that he'd been asking the same question over and over again.

"I don't know," I mumbled running my hand across my forehead in an exasperated manner as my body swayed. "I-I...I don't know."

I wanted him open a side door to the club and I felt his hands harshly grab me by my arms. The security guard threw me out of the club spewing words that I couldn't make out in my dazed stumper. My body landed against someone's car as the door closed behind me. All I could do was lay there hugging the metal of the automobile and praying that my head would stop spinning. I must have passed out for a while because when I came to the only person in sight was a little homeless lady pushing a buggy in my direction.

Quickly I rose up off of the car and glanced around. I began to panic. I had no clue what to do next and no idea where I was exactly. I couldn't even remember how I'd gotten separated from the group or how I'd ended up sprawled across some car in what looked like a back alley. "This is crazy," I muttered to myself as I tried to smooth out and pull down the mini skirt that I was wearing. *Where are my sisters*, I wondered? *How could they have let me get away from them?*

I watched as the frail homeless lady approached me. "Honey," her voice cackled as she spoke. "You looking for some services or did they throw you out the club for drugs?

I sobered up in two seconds. "No ma'am," I responded defensively to both scenarios.

All of a sudden a lot of more homeless people came creeping around the corner. Unsure of what was about to happen next, I took off my shoes, ran up to the side door in front of me, and started banging as hard as I could hope that the bouncer or anyone on the other side would hear me.

"Honey, nobody gonna' let you in," the woman said from right behind me. "They thinking it's one of us banging on their door and they surely don't care about us."

Afraid to walk through the small mob of homeless people to make my way around to the main street and the front entrance of the club, with mixed feelings I said a quick prayer and banged even harder. As if hearing my mental plea another security guard roughly pushed opened the door.

"What you want?" he barked at me.

Nervously, I showed him the club stamp on my arm. "Please sir, let me back in. I'm lost. I don't even know how I got out here. I'm not from here and—"

He grabbed me by my arm and pulled me back into the club nearly yanking the breath out of me and cutting off the end of my rant.

"Thank you very much sir," I said graciously with tears in my eyes. "Thank you!"

J, my sisters, brother-in-law's, and friend came out of nowhere, each screaming at me over the loud music.

"What happened to you? Where did you go?" J hollered the loudest.

I tried to explain what had happened to the best of my memory but, since so much was fuzzy to me my story was making no sense. My attempt to explain only infuriated my boyfriend further. He was so upset that he didn't even want to talk to me. He held his hand up to silence me as I continued to stamper. "Just be quiet," he ordered. "We'll talk about it later."

The others sensed the sternness in his tone and began to make their way towards the main exit. I was hurt. As he pulled my arm to lead me out of the club,

I resisted. He turned to look at me with a questioning glare.

"Aren't you at least glad to know that I'm safe?" I was curious to know. I still didn't how long I'd been outside unconscious and how long the others had been looking for me.

His voice sounded really shaky and I could tell that fear was running through his body. "Melissa, I love you and I don't want anything to happen to you. I told you not to leave my sight. I told you!" His tone was escalated and he stopped himself before going any further. After a deep breath, he squeezed my hand and looked into my eyes. "Understand this… please don't ever do that again."

I felt bad for having worried him and wanted nothing more than to move past this unpleasant part of our trip. I nodded my understanding and allowed him to finally lead me out of the club. So much for my night out in Atlanta, I thought as J escorted me back to our vehicle.

***

The morning before we were scheduled to leave Atlanta J received a call via his cell from a Louisiana number. “It’s my mom,” he told me as he answered the phone. “Hello. Wait a minute, wait a minute. Ma, slow down. What happened?”

I turned over in bed and looked at the rigidness of his face. His body instantly tensed up as he sat up right and kicked his legs over the side of the bed.

“Okay, let me work some things out,” he said, his voice starting to sound muffled. “I’ll call you back in a few.” He disconnected the call and laid the phone down on the bed beside him.

I saw his shoulders slump over and I knew in that moment that something earth shattering had occurred. I rose to my knees and hugged my man from the back as his body shook with tears. “What’s the matter, baby?” I asked. “What happened.”

“My grandmother,” he sobbed. “My grandmother…she…oh god!”

He didn’t have to finish the statement. I assumed that a death had occurred by the way he had immediately broken down. I squeezed him tighter so that he would know I was right there for him as his emotional support system.

"She raised me," he said. "She was my rock. I don't understand."

I kissed the back of his head and stroked the side of his face. "God's plan is not for us to understand," I informed him. A few moments passed as I cradled him in my arms. "You're going fly out to Louisiana? I'm sure you want to be with your family now."

"What about you?" he countered.

The question stunned me. What about me? Why was that a factor when his family was in the midst of a traumatic situation? "I'll be fine, honey. I can fly back home by myself and—"

"No!" he said boldly. "You're not going to do that."

My hand ceased in the stroking motion across his left cheek and I blinked hard trying to understand his position. "Umm…okay. Well, we can get our flight home changed to a later flight and I can just stay here while you go be with your family."

He shook his head. "No," he whispered. "I'm not going. I'm just going to stay here with you and we can fly home together as planned." He grabbed my hands and held them tightly in his with my arms around his neck and my chest pressed hard against his back.

I couldn't understand why he would choose to forego being with his family. It was clear to me that money wasn't an issue for him. Since we were already in the United States it should have been a breeze for him to get a flight from Atlanta to Baton Rouge but he was choosing not to. I wasn't sure if this was the part where I was supposed to insist upon him going and offer to accompany him, but I didn't feel it would be proper for me to intrude upon such a private and emotional family moment. That was no way for me to meet his family for the first time. I decided not to press the issue. This was something that J was going to have to live with on his own, a decision that he would have to come to terms with.

Our Atlanta vacation came to a sullen end as he spent the rest of our last day crying, moaning, and sulking. Charlene had entertained the idea of throwing us a party before we left but, given the circumstances we both agreed that it was best to not do so. Despite the club fiasco and J's grandmother's sudden death, I enjoyed our vacation and I appreciated J for making it possible. But, like all good things, it had to come to an end and it was time for us to get back to our regular lives.

***

Upon returning back to Germany jet lag was a huge issue for me. I only had one day to rest up before having to return back to work. All I wanted to do was sleep. I went to work the following Monday and fell asleep at the desk less than two hours into my shift. The feel of something pointy sticking me in my back jolted me awake. Quickly, I sat upright, but Nadia, my manager, had already caught me.

"You didn't get enough rest on vacation?" she asked.

Embarrassed from being caught off task, I smoothed out my hair and readjusted myself in my chair. "Trying to get re-acclimated to the time change I guess." It was the only excuse that I could think of.

"Mmmhmm. Something's different about you. You've been dragging about since you got here and I'd agree with that time change thing if you had bags under your eyes or something…but no…I think there's something more." She opened a bag of sour cream and onion potato chips and mindlessly placed a few in her mouth as she went on. "Get up and move around a bit. Maybe it'll make you feel better. Whatever will keep you from sleeping at my desk."

The scent of her chips drift up my nose and instantly I covered my mouth, feeling nausea zip through my body. I wrinkled up my nose and frowned at her chips.

"What's the matter?" she asked, looking down at the bag.

"I don't know. Those smell really loud."

She nodded her head. "Yeah, I think you should go get yourself checked out, Melissa. Something's not right with you." She looked at her watch and then pulled down the clipboard containing the schedules of all the security firm's employees at that location. "Go ahead and go home. Take care of yourself and come back refreshed tomorrow. I'll have your shift covered."

"That's not necessary. I just—"

"You're not gonna be sitting here the whole time dozing and vomiting. Now go."

Her word was final so, I grabbed my belongings, clocked out and made my way to my car. As I reached for my keys a notion hit me. Could I be pregnant? There were times when J and I had neglected using contraception. The thought of getting pregnant had never occurred to me until that very moment. Fatigue and nausea were clear signs that my new fear was a very real possibility. Hurriedly, I got into my car, pulled out my cell phone, and then called my doctor's office to make an appointment. I needed to know what was going on with me as soon as possible and I hoped to God that it turned out to be nothing.

Two days later I was sitting on the edge of the exam table waiting for the doctor to return with my lab results. My legs swung back in forth in anticipation as I waited to hear what she had to say. What was only minutes seemed like an eternity before Dr. Schultz finally sauntered into the exam room.

She gave me a reassuring smile. “Well don’t look like I’m about to issue you a death sentence,” she joked.

I smiled nervously. “Just my nerves,” I stated, wringing my hands together.

She looked down at my chart as she took a seat in the chair directly across from me. “Well, your urine test came back positive for HCG hormone indicating a pregnancy. Judging by your report of your last period I estimate you to be around nine weeks of gestation. I want to go ahead and get you scheduled for an ultrasound and get you going on prenatal vitamins.”

With every word she spoke my heart sank deeper into my stomach. I couldn’t believe that it was true, but even more to the point I couldn’t believe that I’d made it a little past two months being pregnant and hadn’t even realized it.

"Do you have any questions for me?" Dr. Schultz asked.

"Nine weeks," I repeated the last thing that I'd actually heard her say. "Are you sure?"

"Well, once we send your blood to the lab and do an ultrasound we'll have a more accurate look at the gestational age, but if you're right about your last period then it should be pretty accurate."

I'd missed a period but I hadn't really been concerned. Over the years that had happened to me quite a few times and it was of no consequence. But now things were different. Now there was a life growing inside of me. I touched my belly and almost cried. *I'm in no shape to be anyone's mother right now*, I thought. *I'm not ready for this*. At the time it was very hard to see myself becoming a mother. So many questions started to flood my head and then the ultimate one came to mind making me shutter at the thought. *What is J going to say?*

***

I went over it and over it in my mind for two days. I hadn't told a soul. This wasn't something that

I was sure I wanted to get myself involved in but I knew that time was running out for me to decide to terminate the pregnancy. Convinced that I was at a point in my life where a baby was just not an option, I was pretty certain that I was going to have to do the unthinkable. But, my conscience wouldn't let me make the appointment or the decision without consulting with J first. I knew that I owed him that much. I strongly believe in karma so the ramifications of doing something this serious and traumatic without his knowledge scared me.

"Babe?"

I heard him calling me as I sat on his sofa and lost somewhere between my thoughts and my fears. "Huh?"

"I asked you which movie you wanted to watch," he said, holding two DVD cases up to my face.

"Oh." I curled up on one end of the sofa and shook shrugged. "It doesn't matter." It really didn't. No matter which movie he played my mind was sure to be elsewhere.

He made a choice on his own and tossed the losing DVD onto the coffee table. "What's up with you?" he asked, as he put the winning DVD in the DVD player. "You've been unusually quiet and kinda aloof."

I bit my bottom lip. My stomach churned from nervousness rather than the morning sickness I seemed to be battling all day every day. It was either now or never. Since he was inquiring about what was up I figured it was the perfect time to share the news. Besides, I didn't know when I'd ever muster up the nerve again. "Umm, we need to talk."

He turned to face me and frowned. "Man! Whenever a woman starts a sentence with those words it can't be a good thing."

He was already prepared for the worse and I wasn't sure how that made me feel. "I haven't really been feeling well," I said. "So I went to the doctor to see what's going on."

"Everything okay?" he asked with his voice laced with concern.

I shrugged. "If you consider being pregnant okay," I said softly while staring him dead in the eyes.

He studied me long and hard before responding as if the realization was taking a little time to actually register in his brain. "Are you serious? Are you telling me you're pregnant, Melissa?"

I held tight to a throw pillow, preparing myself for the fallout. I nodded. "That's what I'm saying."

He threw his hands up in the air and I flinched. I just knew that he was about to hit the roof but was stunned to see him raise his eyes to the heavens as if praying. Once he looked back at me I could clearly see the tears trailing down his face.

"I can't believe this," he said, walking over and kneeling before me. He placed his hands on my stomach and stared at it as if he could actually see evidence of the baby. "I can't believe this. This is the greatest blessing in the world, Melissa." He was happy.

I was torn. How could I tell him that I was thinking about aborting the baby that he seemed to be falling in love with by the second? I placed my hands on top of his trying my best to get up the courage to forge ahead with all that I wanted to say. I opened my mouth to speak but was silenced by his declaration.

"I love you more than the air I breathe," he said. "Everything about us feels right to me, Melissa. And this…" He patted my stomach, pursed his lips, and shook his head. "This is proof that we belong together…that we were destined to be a family." He pulled my hands into his, blinked away his tears, and looked me in the eyes. "Marry me, Melissa. I love you and I want to give you and our baby the world. Please marry me."

I was speechless. This wasn't exactly the way I thought his second proposal would go but what could I do about it? I knew that I loved him and I expected him to pop the question again following our adventures in looking at engagement rings. What I didn't expect was that the proposal would be tied to the fact that I was bearing his child unexpectedly. I took a deep breath and did the only thing that I felt was right. "Yes," I said. "I'll marry you."

~ Chapter 3~
Marriage

"""Men marry women with the hope they will never change. Women marry men with the hope they will change. Invariably they are both disappointed."

Once the decision was made I wanted to hurry up and get the wedding plans started so that I wouldn't be super huge on my wedding day. I diligently researched everything we needed to do prior filing for our marriage license. Once we had all of our paperwork together, we eagerly went down to City Hall to get the process started. We chatted idly with nervous grins as we filled out the documents that the clerk handed to us—J completed his portion and I completed mine. Thereafter, we both signed on the dotted lines and returned the papers at the appropriate window. We stood there patiently waiting for further instructions as the clerk checked over our forms.

"I have papers now that say you're going to be mine," J joked.

I swatted his arm playfully. "No, you signed a paper that says I may end up being yours. Now, once we actually get a signed marriage certificate that's another story."

The clerk raised her eyes over her glasses and spoke in a matter-of-fact tone. "Sir, may I have the copy of your divorce decree?"

My heart stopped beating and the world stood still for what felt like an eternity. Just hearing her say that one simple word—divorce—I felt like a knife had sliced through my body tearing my heart and spirit in half. Surely there was some mistake. I hadn't looked over his portion of the forms so I had no clue what he'd written but I just knew that he couldn't have possibly indicated that he was divorced. The clerk had to have been mistaken.

"I'm sorry, maybe there was an error," I said shaking my head while looking at her although my voice sounded completely unsure.

She didn't even bother to respond to me. She just kept her eyes fixated on J with her hand held out expectantly.

I looked over at him as he stood next to me fiddling quietly and nervously. "J?" I called his name questioningly. The fact that he had yet to deny it should have been evidence enough but I needed to hear him say something. I needed to hear him tell her that it was a mistake.

I watched as he pulled an envelope from his book bag and slid it through the window to the magistrate clerk. My eyes bored holes into that envelope and I stared widely as the clerk pulled out the document she needed and moved forward with processing our request.

"You've been married before?" I asked meekly, hurt dripping from each syllable that left my mouth.

He nodded. "Yes. For about six months."

I was shocked. I looked over at the clerk quickly with in an embarrassed glance knowing full well that she was listening to our every word. Her facial expression as she briefly made eye contact with me read surprise. I figured she was shocked to hear that his marriage had only lasted for half a year whereas I was completely floored to learn that there'd been a wife before me.

"Why are you just now telling me this?" I asked J in a whispered rant. "How could you bring me down here to file for a marriage license knowing they were going to ask you about your previous marriages? Couldn't you have prepared me for this?"

"Okay!" the clerk cut in, handing us back our paperwork and the receipt for the license. "You're all good to go here. Best of luck to you."

Best of luck, I thought. We were going to need every bit of luck we could find because I was more disappointed at that moment than I'd ever been in life. J stuffed the paperwork into his book bag, grabbed my hand, and led me out of the door. I followed quietly and obediently as my thoughts swarmed around my head driving me insane with confusion and frustration. Once we got into his car I was determined to get answers. "So?" I asked.

He started up the car and backed out of his parking spot. "So what?"

"So are you going to tell me why you kept this part of your life a secret?"

He shrugged. "I didn't feel that it was important."

I couldn't believe him. "Not important? You can't be serious, J! It's a part of your life, your history. It's very important."

"No, it's really not. It lasted all of six months. There's no story there. It didn't impact my life in any way. It was a mistake and it's over."

I ignored the finality in his tone. "What happened between you and her?"

"Drop it, Melissa!"

I stared at his face and took in the way his jaw bones tightened and his nostrils flared. He was the one who had kept a secret and embarrassed me yet there he was getting angry because I was questioning him about it. My inquiries were legit. Any other fiancée would want to know that her intended had been married previously. What woman wouldn't want to know how the marriage fell apart or what the other woman was like? "Do you still love her? I mean, was it a catastrophic ending? Did she break your heart?"

"We got married, it didn't work, we got divorced. That's just it!" he snapped.

I opened my mouth to respond and felt a rush of heated anger zip through my body. The baby kicked and I sat back in my seat with my mouth closed, caressing my tiny, protruding belly. I couldn't allow myself to get upset and stressed out about this. It was apparent to me that he didn't want to discuss it and had no intentions of being honest with me about this part of his past. What could I do about it? It wasn't as if he was still married to the woman. It was over. So, in that moment I decided to just drop it and be thankful that his secret hadn't been much worse.

***

J promised me that we would have a big wedding tailored to my specifications in the United States once I had the baby. He knew that I didn't feel glamorous and exquisite as a bride should on her wedding date since I was nearly five months pregnant and picking up weight. For that reason, we agreed that a courthouse ceremony would be idea for now considering we wanted to be husband and wife prior to giving birth to our miracle. After our license was approved we chose a day to head back down to the courthouse and make it official. We took a small entourage of friends with us. Coincidentally, my friend Bianca was also getting married at the courthouse that day. We decided to make a day of it, attending one another's ceremonies and celebrating our nuptials together afterwards.

During an early dinner we toasted to the new life we would all be leading. I watched as Bianca and her new husband Fredrick gazed into each other's eyes during the toast, wrapping their arms around each other's to sip from their wine glasses like couples did in old Hollywood movies. I'd been watching the way the interacted all afternoon, taking note of the way Fredrick regarded her. Even when Bianca wasn't looking Fredrick smiled at her proudly with such a glow on his face that there was no mistaken that he was in love with her. He walked beside her when we were in motion with his arm linked through hers. He listened to her when she spoke, never cutting her off. I liked them together. I felt genuine happiness radiating through their pores while in their presence.

"Are you ready to order now?" Our waitress was back. We'd sent her away twice claiming to need more time to decide upon which entrees we wanted.

J looked to Fredrick and nodded. "You go ahead."

Fredrick then looked to Bianca. "Babe?"

Bianca took a final glance at her menu and then turned her attention to our waitress. "I'll have the roasted chicken with the rice pilaf and garden vegetables."

"And for you, sir?" the waitress asked the Fredrick.

"I'll take the seafood platter please."

"Your sides?"

"Umm...broccoli and a loaded baked potato."

The waitress jotted down his choices and lifted her eyes towards me.

I looked from her back down to my menu, still not completely sure about what my pregnant taste buds had in mind. “Uhh…well the baby back ribs and—”

“She’ll have the roasted chicken as well with a baked potato, not loaded and put the butter on the side, and broccoli,” J stated, cutting me off. “And for me, I’ll take the rib eye, well done, a loaded potato and broccoli as well. Oh, and a garden salad with Balsamic dressing for my wife here.”

“Okay, I’ll put those orders right in,” the waitress replied. “My I have your menus?”

Bianca and Fredrick handed theirs to her first. She then retrieved J’s and I pursed my lips and avoided her eyes as I turned mine over to her last. It wasn’t the first time he’d ordered for me. At first I found it chivalrous and cute. But the fact that he’d completely overlooked my desires and shut me down as I was speaking for myself rubbed me the wrong way. However, I didn’t say a word. I didn’t want to give Bianca and Fredrick the impression that anything was wrong and I certainly didn’t want to taint the first night of our marriage by arguing in front of our friends. The thought of eating chicken made my stomach turn, but I forged through dinner for the sake of peace. What harm would it cause to allow him to be the man and not refute him in front of others? A good wife was supposed to be submissive to her husband and she definitely wasn't expected to make him look bad in public. With a smile, I ate the meal he chose for me and kept it moving. It was our wedding night. We deserved to be happy.

***

J had moved into my house with me and after saying our 'I do's' at the courthouse, we began to settle into life as a married couple. We now shared the same space and equal responsibility for the expenses we incurred. On the day that he told me he'd decided to get discharged from the military I nearly lost it. His income was generous and because of it we were able to live a nice cushiony lifestyle. I was still working my fulltime job, but I had assumed that I'd eventually let it go and allow my husband to be the breadwinner, as I felt it should be. But, he had it in his mind that he should be a stay-at-home dad. The notion was ridiculous to me. He rarely cleaned up after himself as it was so I knew that there was no way he would really want to stay home day after day tending to the house and caring for the baby once he was born. It just wasn't who J was.

After about a month or two of sitting around bored the tedium quickly wore him out. J decided to get a part time job at a book store.

"Just until the baby comes," he'd explained to me.

Still, I wondered how long he would be able to hang being stuck in the house everyday once the baby was there. He seemed to be content with his bookstore job although he claimed he didn't really like the job. He considered it a means to end temporarily. I noticed that he would come home in good spirits which was a welcomed change from the grumpy being he'd turned into during the short time he'd been unemployed. I wasn't thrilled about working my forty hour a week shift while he worked fifteen to twenty hours, but I appreciated the fact that he would at least have dinner prepared for me most nights to help lighten my load.

Since I'd never been to his job and I wanted to surprise him, one Saturday while having nothing to do, I decided to get myself dolled up and pay him a visit. I figured treating him to lunch would be a good surprise. Plus, I'd get an opportunity to see him in his new element. I threw on a cute little floral maternity dress and sandals, pushed my hair back with a band as my natural tresses hung freely, applied a minimum amount of makeup to help accent the beauty of my pregnancy glow, and headed out to the Read Me Now bookstore in search of my husband.

"May I help you?" a female whose nametag read Crystal asked me.

I shook my head. "I'm just looking for my husband, Jason. He works here."

Crystal gasped. "J is your husband?"

I was a little caught off guard hearing the woman refer to my husband by his nickname. I found it to be overly familiar and unprofessional of her to do so. "Yes," I replied. "He is."

"Oh, okay…well, he's over there helping a customer out in the history section," Crystal stated, waving her hand towards an area on the other side of the store though her eyes never left my belly. "You want me to go get him for you or—"

"No, I'll find him," I insisted, cutting her insincere offer short. "Thank you." I turned my back to her before she could say another word and waddled my way over to J.

He saw me just as I approached the history section and his eyes crinkled up at the corners as he smiled. "Is there anything else I can help you with?" he asked the gentleman whom he was assisting.

"No, no. I think that's it," the man replied.

"Hey, babe!" I exclaimed as J tore himself away from his customer and approached me.

He embraced me tightly and kissed my cheek. "What are you doing here?" He rubbed my stomach lovingly. "Everything okay?"

"Everything's fine. I just thought I'd pop in and surprise you. I want to take you to lunch."

"Oh," he said hesitantly. "Well, that is a surprise."

I didn't understand his tone. For a moment it felt as if he wasn't pleased by the idea of having lunch with me. I didn't know whether to feel hurt that he didn't want to spend that time with me or pissed that I'd wasted my time and energy coming down there only to be shot down by my husband.

"Come on," he said, grabbing my hand. "I want you to meet my co-workers."

He'd informed me upon starting the job that majority of his team members were females. As he led me back to the customer care counter in the middle of the store where three other women had joined Crystal and were all staring shamelessly in our direction, I wanted nothing less than to go and stand before those barracudas. I knew that they were discussing me as we moved closer. The moment he placed me front and center they would waste no time in scrutinizing me from head to toe.

"Hey everybody, I want you to meet my wife," J announced as we stood face to face with his team members. He put one arm around me in what felt like a protective hold. I guessed that he too assumed these women would try to pick me apart.

"Hi," they all sang in unison with phony smiles plastered to their faces.

"It's nice to meet you," the one in the middle stated. "I'm Lori. This is Bre and Karmen," she said pointing to the women to her right. "And you've already met Crystal."

Crystal gave me yet another plastic smile as she toyed with her braids. Her eyes shot over to J and then back to me as if sizing up our compatibility.

"It's nice to meet you all as well," I replied. *Yea right*, I thought. I really wanted to tell those trolls that they had better stay away from my husband, but I was far too classy to allow myself to be anything other than ladylike. I let out an exasperated breath and felt J give me a little squeeze.

"You two heading out for lunch?" Crystal asked with that stupid look still on her face.

"Uh, seems like that's the plan," J replied. He looked at me and noticed my troubled expression. "You okay, babe?"

"Just a little out of breath," I told him.

"How about we just grab something from the café instead of going out somewhere," he suggested.

I smiled politely seeing that the other women were standing there watching us like we were a soap opera. I didn't want to stay another second in that store with those vultures hounding us, but I didn't want to make a scene either. Besides, it was getting increasingly difficult for me to move around and I was already out of breath. On top of that I knew that sitting anywhere for a long period of time would be uncomfortable so it was probably just best to stay there and have a quick bite so that I could get back home to my comfortable bed. "Okay," I told him. "Lead the way." *Get me away from these women before I scratch someone's eyes out*, I thought.

J took my hand and led me to the café.

"Enjoy your lunch!" Crystal called out.

I noticed that J didn't bother to respond or turn around. However, I managed to glance back and there was no mistaking the glare in her eyes and the snarl upon her lips. I wasn't pleased. I figured that the women flirted with J seeing as though he was the only man that worked their shift, but something in Crystal's attitude told me that something a little more than harmlessly flirting was going on. Did this chick really have the audacity to be crushing on my husband? Asking J about it would be pointless. Men were sometimes so oblivious to things like a woman throwing herself at him. But, if Crystal knew what was best for her she'd stay in her lane. I didn't really have the energy to be making frequent trips to Read Me Now.

***

I was exhausted. My body couldn't take any more of the torture that the baby was inflicting upon me internally. By October 16, 2005 my son was officially two weeks overdue and I was ready to pass out. Sitting in the car as J drove us to the hospital for my scheduled C-section, I didn't know what bothered me the most—the discomfort of carrying around an abnormally large baby or the anxiety of being cut up in order to get him out of me. My nerves were shot. Thoughts of whether I'd survive the routine procedure drove me mad. Worries about whether or not I was fit to be a mother still consumed me. I clutched the arm of the door as I stared blankly out of the window while trying to settle my emotions.

"You planning on jumping out of the car?" J asked, laughing at his own humor.

I rolled my eyes. "Ha, ha." I was in no mood for jokes. In a few hours our lives were about to change once the tiny being was placed in my arms. Meanwhile, my body had reached its limit and was screaming to be set free.

The rest of our ride to the hospital became a blur as I prayed and tried to keep my tears of fear at bay. J ushered me into the maternity ward and the hospital staff tended to us accordingly. By the time I made it into the sterile environment of the operating room my nerves had gone into overdrive. I was shaking uncontrollably and my breathing was so unregulated that the scrub nurses were afraid for me.

"Honey, are you okay?" a nurse with thick glasses asked me.

I couldn't answer. About the only thing that I could do without fainting or falling into a hysterical fit was nod and cry.

"No you're not," she said, looking at me cautiously and holding on to my arm as I stood in front of the operating table. “You’re not okay. You’re going to get yourself all worked up and then end up shooting your blood pressure sky high. What’s the matter?”

I looked around the room and felt my resolve weakening. This was not the way I’d planned to give birth to my first child—in an operating room with machinery everywhere as a result of being so horribly uncomfortable for so long. This wasn’t the way childbirth was depicted in the movies or any of the shows I’d watch to prepare me for the moment. This looked like the beginning of a nightmare.

“You’re scared?” the nurse asked.

Another nurse who had just finished scrubbing and dressing in her surgical attire stood just a few feet away from us watching. “Lord, I think she’s gonna’ pass out. Nel, she needs oxygen! Give her oxygen!”

“Here, sit down.” Nel, the first nurse instructed me. She guided me onto the operating table before reaching over to her left and retrieving an oxygen mask. She placed it over my mouth and nose and looked into my eyes. “Come on, honey. Breathe deeply and calmly. You've gotta calm down, sugar. This isn't good for you or your baby."

"Is she okay?" I heard another nurse ask.

"I don't know," the second nurse answered. "I think she's going to have a panic attack. I told Nel to give her oxygen. Poor thing."

"Dr. Kates is ready to come in and do the epidural."

My eyes grew wide with fear at the mention of the local anesthesia. I'd already been given an explanation of how that procedure worked and the thought of the needle being inserted in my spine was exactly what I needed at that moment to drive me over the edge. My body began to convulse and Nel grabbed me in a tight embrace.

"What you doing?" the third nurse asked.

"Body pressure," Nel explained. "It helps calm a person down when they're panicking."

The other two nurses walked over and joined in the embrace, each cooing and trying their best to calm me down. Together they prayed for me and my baby and after a while I felt myself begin to relax. What they'd done was completely out of hospital protocol but they'd done it anyway. The fact that they cared enough about my mental, emotional, and physical wellbeing to risk being written up for embracing me and for the religious encounter meant the world to me. Finally, I was able to allow them to lay me down and hook me up to the necessary monitors before Dr. Kates came in to administer my epidural. Nurse Nel held my hand through the process.

Once my lower half grew numb the rest of the experience was a breeze. My doctor, Dr. Schultz, came into the room in high spirits and it took all of fifteen minutes before I heard a slap and then the wail of my beautiful baby boy. Another half an hour ensued as they removed the placenta and sewed me up while cleaning my baby just across the floor from me. From my position all I could see was the ceiling and the backs of the nurses as they fiddled around with my son. I was anxious to lay eyes on him, to hold him in my arms for the very first time.

As if hearing my thoughts and sensing my impatience, Nel brought the baby over to me tightly bungled up in the standard hospital blankets. "Are you ready for your little one, Mom?" she asked me.

I outstretched my arms and she placed him securely in the bend of my elbow. Immediately, I held on to him like as if I'd never see him again. His face was bright yellow, devoid of pigmentation just yet. His head full of beautiful, slick, black hair intrigued me. His eyes fluttered yet barely opened. In that moment I fell deeper in love than I ever knew I could be. For twenty-six inches and weighing ten pounds my son appeared almost as big in person as he felt inside of my body. Originally Dr. Schultz had planned to induce my labor after the baby hadn't budged upon approaching my due date, but following a final ultra sound she decided against it due to the baby's positioning and the guesstimated size of his skull. However, looking at my perfect angel for the first time his head didn't appear to be that big to me at all.

"Wow." J's voice caused me to jerk my head to the right in his direction. I hadn't even noticed him being brought into the room. "Look at him," he said.

"It's nothing short of amazing, huh?" I replied. For so long I'd been fretting over the decision to go through with my pregnancy, afraid that motherhood wasn't exactly something that was designed for me. But, holding my son in my arms, watching the peace that surrounded him, feeling his heartbeat, smelling the sweet scent that was his very own I knew without a doubt that no other decision could have ever been correct. We were destined to be together, my son and I. Despite the discomfort I'd endured and the anxiety over the C-section the feeling of being a mother was awesome. I couldn't believe that it was actually happening.

"Hey Trey," J said softly, touching the baby's fine hair. "Hey son."

I looked into J's eyes and felt so much love that I just knew our lives would be forever blessed.

***

By the time Trey and I returned home from the hospital, my husband had everything ready. He'd been working tirelessly in the baby's room for months during his off days—painting, putting together the crib, baby swing, and a few toys. His proud father persona was apparent in the way he smiled widely and carefully handled Trey as he so much as carried the baby in his car seat from the car to his room. I was exhausted and wanted nothing more than to lay in my comfortable bed as still as possible to keep from aggravating the stiches that were holding my skin together.

I walked slowly behind J as he entered Trey's room. From the doorway I watched as my husband gently unclasped the buckles of the car seat and lifted out our tiny miracle. Trey fussed a little during the transfer.

"Okay, okay," J cooed as he carried the baby in a rather awkwardly stiff position over to the changing table. "I'm gonna make sure you're dry, give you some warm milk, and lay you over in your bed fit for a prince. Okay buddy?" He proceeded to change our son for the first time. His movements were all hesitant and slow but he accomplished the task.

I continued watching them feeling touched to witness the early father-son bond. I felt so warm and content and was immediately overwhelmed by the love I felt for our family. For the next three months of my maternity leave I was able to relish in the life that we'd created. Nothing was better than watching all of the cute things Trey did and becoming acclimated with parenthood. Together J and I tag-teamed with regards to changing and feeding the baby day and night. We worked well together and I appreciated the times that he would give me extra time to rest and doing nothing while he and Trey did their own thing.

Before we knew it my maternity leave was over and it was time for me to return to work. I was a little pensive about leaving J on his own to tend to the baby. We'd both grown accustomed to working together to care for the child and now he'd be doing it alone. On day one I expected to come home and find the house in disarray but was pleasantly surprised to see that J was able to manage well enough to not only clean the house and take care of Trey, but he also had a full dinner waiting on me upon my arrival. *Maybe this arrangement will work for us*, I thought at the time. Soon after, I realized that just because someone was capable of doing something didn't mean that it was something they were happy with doing.

Three months into his stay-at-home-dad career, J broke. I'd just arrived home from work and was completely exhausted. The moment I opened the door I knew that it wasn't going to be a peaceful night like the ones I was used to coming home to. The baby was crying loudly via the baby monitor sitting on the coffee table and J was in the kitchen hollering about a pot of peas that had apparently burned judging by the scorched scent that assaulted my nose. My motherly instinct was to hurry to Trey's room and lift him out of the crib where he lay on his back with his tiny fists balled up in frustration accompanying his shrill cries. The moment he felt my touch and inhaled my scent his wails turned into a mere whimper and the frigidness of his body loosened up as he cozied up to my chest.

"What's the matter with Mama's big little man, huh?" I cooed, rocking him lovingly as I headed back up the hall towards the kitchen. "What's the matter? You smelling that stinky stuff, huh?"

"Forget it!" J tossed the pot of burned beans into the sink just as we entered the kitchen. After it he tossed the spoon that he'd been using to scoop out the peas that he felt were salvageable.

"What's going on?" I asked, looking around my kitchen at the wreck that had occurred.

Empty vegetable cans, scraps of paper, cutlery, and empty, bloody meat trays met my glare. The stench in the room combined with the clutter made me want to turn around and walk right back out of the house.

"I was trying to cook dinner but you see how that turned out," J responded with irritation as he motioned turned the destroyed pot. "Baby been crying all day for no reason."

"Did you change him?"

"Of course I changed him, Melissa. I'm not stupid."

I rocked the baby and ignored J's tone. "When was his last bottle?"

"An hour ago? What? You think I don't know what he needs? I've done everything for him, Melissa. Maybe he just wants you."

"Aww. He just wants a little T.L.C," I cooed as I looked into my son's beautiful eyes.

Trey cosigned my assumption with a gummy grin that made my heart melt.

"Well, I can't sit around just holding him all day. That's going to make him a spoiled child and nobody wants to deal with a bratty baby. I have other things to do around him rather than just coddle him all day, Melissa."

"I didn't say coddle him all day. I said…oh never mind. Here, I'll tend to Trey and you can finish dinner," I suggested.

He waved me off and huffed. "I can't do this anymore."

I was alarmed. My glance went from the baby to his father as I metered my tone carefully. "What do you mean?"

He waved his arms around frantically. "This! I can't do this anymore. This staying home and taking care of the house and baby business. I'm going crazy. Feeling unproductive and defeated at the same time. I need something more."

"Okay…okay. Well, maybe we can find you a decent job with some flexible hours."

"I gotta go back to what I know…what makes me happy emotionally and financially."

I pretty much saw where he was going with his last statement. "Are you saying you want to re-enlist?" The thought of him having to deploy and leaving me behind with a new baby to take care while trying to work and maintain our home didn't really sit well with me.

"I already put in a call."

My knees buckled and I had to remember that I was holding the baby so that I wouldn't pass out. Conscious of the precious life cradled in my arms, I leaned against the counter for extra support. "You already made the decision? Without talking with me about it first?"

"I don't need your permission."

I was stunned. "I'm not saying that you needed my permission, but we're married now, J. We're a family. You can't just go making decisions that affect the *whole family* without consulting the *rest of* the family."

His eyes narrowed in on me and his teeth gritted as he spoke. "A man is supposed to do whatever he has to take care of his family. I don't need to consult with you on that. Besides, I talked it over with Trey and he didn't have any qualms about the idea," he added sarcastically.

The massive amount of hurt that filled my being couldn't be expressed with words. "So that's just it? You're just going to do it no matter what I think?"

He reached for the empty meat trays and tossed them in the trash. "I think it's best for us," he stated. "You'll be okay. I'm going to go order a pizza." He exited the kitchen leaving me shattered emotionally while holding our son.

I didn't think it was unfair of me to want my husband to make decisions with me about how things in our life would go. But, he'd made it clear that I had no say and it would do me no good to let him know that I was disappointed in how he'd handled the situation. He was a man that assumed complete control. He'd shown me this time and time again. This was just perhaps another one of those times where he was showing me exactly who he was and I had no choice but to believe him.

~ Chapter 4~
U.S.A

"The ache for home lives in all of us. The safe place where we can go as we are and not be questioned."
–Maya Angelou, *All God's Children Need Traveling Shoes*

As if J deciding to re-enlist wasn't bad enough, we were also forced to transfer from Germany to the United States. Fort Carson in Colorado Springs would now be our home. By the time we got the news we had only two weeks before we had to leave. How could I just give up my job, my home, my car, my furniture, and my friends in what seemed like the blink of an eye? I was basically told that I had to leave my entire life behind in order to follow my husband and this whimsical decision that he'd made without my input. I had to really ask myself if I was ready to take that big step towards the next level in our lives. I never expected us to be uprooted from the foundation that I thought we were creating for our family right there in Germany. After lots of praying and thinking I decided that I wanted to keep my family intact and weather whatever storms change would bring our way.

My husband left in March leaving me behind to make some more money so that we would have a good start in the United States. I didn't want us to just pick up everything and move only to be alone in a foreign city struggling with little or nothing. For my birthday in June he sent Trey and I plane tickets to come visit him for two weeks. We landed on the 27th of June. June 28th was my birthday. The time difference of nine hours was very difficult to get used to. My son slept all day long and was wide awake at night upon us settling into the apartment that J had secured for himself. I didn't get any rest the first night that we were there.

Knock, knock, knock. Somebody was banging on the door the next morning pulling me out of the slumber that I'd fitfully fallen into in the wee hours of the morning. Groggily, I climbed out of bed and drug myself to the front door. J had already left for his post for the day and Trey was sound asleep in the playpen erected in the bedroom.

Knock, knock, knock. The visitor was impatiently banging on the door as I finally approached. Who could be coming to J's place anyway, I wondered. Looking through the peephole I could see the delivery guy holding a vase of flowers with an agitated expression on his face. Immediately I remembered that it was my birthday and I flung open the door.

"Melissa?" he questioned with an annoyed tone.

I nodded and reached for the vase.

"Enjoy," he stated as he turned away and quickly disappeared.

I shut the door and sniffed the fragrance of the beautiful floral arrangement filled with white roses and purple tiger lilies. A small card rested in the prongs of a plastic stick. I anxiously snatched it out and flipped it open to read the inscription.

Be ready by 6. –J

My smile spread widely across my face and in that instant I realized how much I'd really missed my husband. The days of him sweeping me off of my feet and surprising me seemed to be so long gone considering our brief separation, but now we were in the same place and he was obviously preparing to make my birthday memorable. I spent the remainder of the day glowing with anticipation as I cared for Trey and lazed about the home that I was unfamiliar with. As the time grew nearer for J to pick us up I bathed and dressed Trey and then took extra care in making sure that I looked my best for whatever it was that J had in store for us.

We had an early dinner at a gorgeous Chinese restaurant like none other than I'd ever visited. Following dinner, he showed me around Colorado Springs. I felt like a true tourist but I had to admit that it was a beautiful city. In some ways the atmosphere reminded me a lot of Germany. Our next stop was a lavish looking plaza with lots of boutiques in it that gave me the impression that they serviced high-end clientele.

"Get whatever you want, babe," he told me as we slowly walked around one of the exquisite shops.

He did not have to tell me twice. His willingness to splurge on me reminded me of our visit to Atlanta when he'd gone above and beyond supplying me with all of my heart's desires. Upon his declaration, I exited the clothing store and bee lined for the nearby shoe store. While I was checking out some fly shoes that had caught my attention the moment I entered the store, I noticed a strange lady walk up to my husband.

"Hey, J," she said nonchalantly with a smile.

I put down the shoe and moved to stand beside him. I gave the woman a look of disdain and then turned my expression over to J. "Excuse me, but who is she?"

"Just the girl of one of the guys I'm cool with," he answered.

The woman opened her mouth to speak and then quickly closed it as if giving it a second thought. "Enjoy the rest of your evening," she said before walking off.

I wasn't fooled. Attitude was bouncing off of that woman and resentment rang through her tone as she bid us farewell. I knew that J had injured himself during a basketball game during the first month that he'd been living in Colorado Springs. During the time of his treatment he'd been on medical leave from work which lasted roughly a month. I assumed that he used that time to get to know a few people that he now claimed to be cool with. I wondered if the woman who had just sashayed away from us was one of the people he'd taken the time to get to know during his brief period off from work. I watched her until she disappeared from my line of vision and then once again I looked to my husband.

"What?" he asked defensively.

I didn't believe the explanation he'd given me but I decided not to make a big deal out of it. I took a deep breath and walked away to revisit the shoe that had originally caught my attention. But, the truth of the matter was that my enthusiasm over shopping had diminished as a result of running into J's little friend. After browsing a little while longer and purchasing nothing, we returned home. So much for my birthday.

Trey became my best friend during our visit with J. While J was working and even when he was home, Trey and I did everything together. We fell into a routine that was all our own—cleaning, playtime, cooking, naptime, play time, and then daddy came home and we'd either engage with him or take to the living room where we played, watched T.V., and then prepared for bed. I started to feel like a real housewife and I wondered if this was what life was going to be like once we finally made the move to live there permanently.

Our two-week visit went by quickly. Before we knew it was time to head back to Germany. A part of me felt relieved to be returning to my own environment since our visit had been rather uneventful. J took the day off to spend our last day with us. Our flight was scheduled to leave that evening. We spent the day at the movies and playing with Trey. Close to time for takeoff J hung out at the airport with us. He lingered at the terminal until the moment it was time to say goodbye. Before Trey and I headed to get in line to board the plane I took a final look at my husband. The look on his face gave me goose bumps. He looked so sad that my heart began to ache for him. Tears began to roll down his face.

"You're coming right back, right?" he asked pathetically.

In that moment he must have realized how much he missed having us around while we were clear across the world. The sincerity and fear of losing us that I heard in his voice was enough to soften my heart and make me forget of the misgivings I'd been feeling for the duration of my visit. "Give me a little more time to get everything together," I told him before placing a small kiss upon his trembling lips.

He kissed his son and took a final look at his family before nodding his understanding. "Call me when you make it home," he instructed.

I carried Trey in my arms and filed into the line to board our plane. From behind me I could hear J telling me that he loved me but by the time the attendant checked my ticket I was unable to see him through the crowd upon turning around to get a last glimpse of him. Sullenly, I followed the path leading to the aircraft, found my seat, and get situated for the flight home. Trey slept for the full duration of the fifteen-hour travel time. I slept off and on, but mostly I remembered the hurt look in J's face as we parted ways.

Upon returning home and trying to settle back into our usual routine I felt my soul begin to ache daily. I missed my husband and I felt horrible thinking about how he must have been struggling to get through each day as well. J called us every evening around 6:00 PM. I made sure to never miss those calls. It was the only time that we had to bond and get caught up on what was going on in the other's life. The long distance relationship was beginning to take a toll on us and by the end of July I'd decided that I just couldn't take the separation any longer. After talking about it with J the arrangements were made and he secured Trey and I plane tickets to return to him indefinitely on September 4th. It was a bittersweet occasion for me since that was also the date of my mother's birthday. It pained me to be leaving her behind in Germany, especially on her birthday. But it pained me more on a daily basis to be living so far apart from my husband. It just wasn't right.

Before leaving for Colorado Springs my friends threw me a surprise going away party. It too was bittersweet. They were happy for me to be taking a leap and moving on to the next stage of my life, but they too were sad to see me go. My mother was in attendance and used every possible opportunity to let me know that she was always there for me no matter what. I took it as her just being concerned about her baby girl going off to embark upon a new journey in building her family. I understood her sentiments and assured her that everything would be fine, that Trey, J, and I would have a new wonderful life in Colorado Springs. I don't know if I was trying to convince my mother or myself.

***

The first two months that Trey and I lived in Colorado Springs went by quickly. It was a rather smooth transition and everything was wonderful. We fell into the same routine that we'd adopted during our previous visit but the relationship between J and I seemed to be strengthened now by the fact that I was there to stay. On Christmas Day we were invited to a Christmas party hosted by one of my husband's co-workers who happened to live across the street from the quaint home that we were renting. After having our own small scale celebration and gift exchange at home, which mainly consisted of gifts for Trey, we got dressed and headed over as a family to join the party. J's co-worker Enrique Rodriquez greeted us at the door and advised that Trey could be placed upstairs in the guest room with the other children who were being watched by Enrique's teenage niece so that the adults could celebrate freely.

It was a nice party with lots of food and drinks. Trey seemed to enjoy being in the midst of the other children. Each time that I checked on him he was either crawling around gaily after a toy or sitting in the middle of the floor staring in awe with a drooling smile at the activity around him. It was my first time actually getting out of the house and meeting new people since we'd moved there. Everyone was so nice including Enrique's wife Amelia Rodriquez who was a very gracious hostess.

At some point J excused himself whispering to me that he had to use the bathroom. I watched him exit the Preston's front door and through the window I saw him head over to our house. I assumed that he had to have a bowel movement and didn't feel comfortable doing so in the Rodríguezes" facilities. About thirty minutes later I went upstairs to check on my son. He was in a play pen whining, cranky from exhaustion. It was well past his bed time. I picked him up as Enrique's niece, Selena, instructed the other children to quiet down as she put a movie into the DVD player and turned the light out so that they could all settle down. Rocking Trey I happened to look up and glance out of the window over to our house. I noticed that there was no light shining from the windows where our bathrooms were located. I found it weird but nothing alerted me to be concerned.

I exited the guest room where the other children were still rather hyper despite the movie that was put on to calm them. In the hallway I ran into Enrique who was just exiting the master bedroom.

"Everything okay?" Enrique asked me, eyeing Trey in my arms.

"Oh yes," I replied. "He's just a little fussy and needs some quiet so he can get to sleep. Is there another room I can lay him down in just until my husband gets back?"

Enrique pointed to the door he'd just come out of. "Sure, sure. You can lay him in our bed. No one will go in there and disturb the little guy. Just use the pillows to put around him to try to keep him from rolling off of the edges."

"Thank you," I said as I headed for the master bedroom door.

"Where is J anyway?" Enrique asked curiously.

Now that he'd asked the question my own worries began to sink in. "Hmmm. That's a good question, sir."

Enrique winced and held his hands up. "Ewww. Please don't call me sir. It's all family in this house."

I smiled at his kindness.

"I mean, you're the only one that's not from Puerto Rico but we still love you." He laughed at his own joke.

I laughed internally at the foolery. *So my husband must have told you that same lie he told me*, I thought. It astonished me how one could be so ashamed of his birthplace that he felt the need to make one up. I thanked Enrique again for his hospitality then entered the master bedroom to lay my son to rest before rejoining the other party-goers downstairs. An hour and a half later J resurfaced. He fed me some bull about how his stomach hurt so badly.

"Do you want to just get Trey and go home?" I asked, looking him dead in the eyes to watch intently as he continued to lie to me.

He shook his head. "I don't want to be rude to Enrique and Amelia," he said. "We can stay. I think I can make it."

Uh-huh, I thought. "Well, Trey's asleep upstairs so I'm gonna run and get his pajamas so he can be more comfortable and another bottle just in case he wakes up hungry."

J nodded. "Okay. That's cool."

"Keep an ear out for him just in case he starts crying up there," I advised. "He's in the room alone."

"Okay, I've got him," he assured me.

I paused for a moment, still looking at J as if giving him the opportunity to tell me the truth. When nothing was forthcoming from him I rose from my seat and left out of the house. I moved swiftly across the street to our home and wasted no time in surveying both of our bathrooms. Just as I suspected each one was in perfect condition—no stench of feces and no scent of recently sprayed air freshener. I was sick to my stomach from the assumptions that began to fill my head. Was J up to the same mess that he'd pulled on me in the past? Feeling woozy I slowly sat down on the closed toilet seat in our master bathroom and remembered the first time I'd felt completely insecure and betrayed.

Two Years Ago…

Back in Germany recently after we'd gotten married everybody was telling me he was cheating on me with my sister's girlfriend. I acted like I didn't believe it and just told them to stop hating. I didn't want anything creating a rift between J and I especially so soon in our relationship. On a night when we were both free and needing to get out, we decided to visit a bar in my hometown. J walked in first with me trailing behind him. My sister's girlfriend, Mercy, stood on the side of the dance floor unable to see me from her position. Mindful of the rumors that I'd heard, I could not wait to see the reaction on her face once he passed her and she saw that he was there with me. The gesture would make my position known thus causing her to back off knowing that she could and would never have him. As he approached the dance floor, Mercy went from sticking out her tongue suggestively to sucking on her lips. Her blatant disrespect was far too much for me to overlook.

"Oh hell no!" I said to myself as I stepped from behind his trailing figure, detoured away from the dance floor, ran through the huge crowd, stepping to the approaching Mercy before she could reach J. Without hesitation, I punched her in her face connecting my fist to her nose.

It happened all so quickly. After the impact I shook my hand from the pain, blinked, and looked down to see her laying on the floor with blood everywhere. I looked at my fist and saw that traces of her blood lingered there as well. Before I could do or say anything else the bar's security guard grabbed me from behind.

"You gotta go!" he shouted.

A crowd had gathered around the scene and for the first time I noticed that I was the center of attention. It was the first time in my life that I had gotten into a fight. It was embarrassing that the experience occurred in my adulthood and nonetheless over a man. There was no other explanation for my actions other than the fact that I'd simply lost it. Seeing her have no respect for our relationship and knowing what everyone was saying behind my back and even to my face about them had led me to act out of character taking my frustrations out on Mercy's face. Although I felt bad about carrying myself in such an unladylike manner in public, I felt vindicated in my actions because of the way Mercy had disrespected me. I spent nearly the whole drive home fuming over Mercy and what she'd done, but by the time we arrived at my house I realized that I shouldn't have lashed out at her. Why wasn't I upset with him? In the back of my mind I even wondered if maybe he'd been the one to pursue her in the first place.

Later, while I was trying to get some sleep he wanted to talk. The last thing I wanted to do was have a discussion with him about anything. I was embarrassed and felt hurt enough. Anything that he could possibly have to say would only serve to make matters worse.

"What is there to talk about?" I asked him, turning my back to him. "Just leave me alone."

"I didn't sleep with her, Melissa," he said in his defense. "I promise you that I never touched that girl."

My mind began to figure out all the ways that his statement could have been true yet false at the same time. "Maybe you didn't have sex with her but you've certainly done something with her," I stated, imagining Mercy's lips around the manhood of the guy lying next to me. I shuddered at the thought and scooted a little further away from him. "Just leave me alone," I reiterated.

"I haven't done anything with her at all, baby. You gotta believe me. I wouldn't do that to you. I just wouldn't."

I felt the tears stinging my eyes as I closed them shut. "Yeah, sure...and the grass is yellow. Whatever," I said sighing. "Good night!" Deep inside I knew that he'd cheated on me with Mercy. I knew that all the things people had been telling me had some level of truth to them. I knew that Mercy wouldn't have dared been so openly sensual and flirty with him if he hadn't given her reason to believe that she had the right to. I knew all of that but I still wanted to believe that he loved me like he claimed he did.

Current Day…Back at the Party…

Shaking off my misgivings yet feeling defeated, I made my way back over to the party. My mind was distracted as I crossed the street, sauntered through the Rodríguezes' front door, and loomed through the sea of guests. I didn't really feel like partying anymore. As I entered the den at the back of the house I saw J standing facing the full wall bookshelf with his back to me. I moved in closer to him and realized that he was speaking to someone on his cell phone. His words were muttered and indecipherable over the chatter in the room, yet as the moment he turned around towards me his face told me all I needed to know. The smile he'd donned while speaking vanished into an expression of pure guilt.

He covered the mouthpiece of his phone and looked at me. "I'm on the line with one of my team members, baby. Give me a second."

"Sure you are," I responded sarcastically before turning around to leave the room. Majority of his coworkers were right there at the party. I couldn't think of anything important enough for him to be on the phone about at this time of night on Christmas. I went upstairs to dress Trey in his pajamas. Midway through the process, J stuck his head in the door.

"Hey, I'm kinda tired so let's go ahead and head home," he said. Before I could respond he left.

I sighed. If that was the case I could have taken Trey home with me and stayed there when I'd left to do the bathroom inspections. J's lack of consideration bothered me and only fueled my contempt for the way our marriage seemed to be going. That night I couldn't sleep. I stared at the ceiling and listened to my conscience tell me that I needed to get out of this relationship. I had no solid proof that he was messing around but my intuition spoke volumes. It saddened me that I'd flown across the world, leaving my family behind, to be with the man that I'd promised to love and cherish forever only to end up feeling trapped and unloved.

The next morning, I was awakened by J stirring around in the room. The sunlight peeked through the windows blinding me as I tried to focus in on his figure standing at the foot of our bed. When I saw the duffle bag on the bed I pulled myself together and sat up to look at him. “Where are you going?”

“To the gym to work out,” he answered. “Gotta work off some of that turkey and stuffing and get my muscles back right.” He gave me a smile and continued stuffing his workout clothes into the duffle bag.

I noticed that he was dressed in jeans and a casual shirt. I found it odd that he would leave for the gym dressed like he was going to hang out instead of just leaving in his workout clothes. I leaned back against my pillows and thought about the fact that he hadn’t too long ago injured his shoulder resulting in him needing surgery to correct it. He’d recently returned to work but was already gung-ho about getting into the gym and lifting weights. I was sure that his doctor hadn’t approved that type of strenuous physical activity just yet. I remained silent as he finished packing, carelessly kissed my cheek, and left our bedroom. I listened as he made his way through the house and finally let himself out of the front door. I didn't budge until after I heard his car start up. Even then I waited a good five minutes to give him the opportunity to pull out of the driveway. Satisfied that he was gone, I hopped out of bed.

The entire ordeal made me sick to my stomach. I felt certain that during his medical leave and being idle and bored with me being in Germany J had met someone that he was messing around with. The notion was clear to me. I just needed proof. I headed to the laundry room where I decided to begin my search. I didn't know what I was looking for or where I'd actually find it either. I just knew that I had to start digging somewhere. I knew that if I went through his stuff I would certainly find something to explain his recently irrational behavior. Standing in front of the clothes hamper I froze up. I was afraid—afraid I would really find something and afraid of what it was that I would find. Feeling weak, I left the laundry room and entered the living room where I sat on the couch and thought.

"You need a plan," I told myself. "You need a course of action. How are you going to handle this?"

I considered approaching him about my suspicions but realized that in doing so I would only make my living situation harder. He was bound to treat me with even more disregard if he knew that I was on to him. I lowered my head in defeat and felt my body grow heavy. This was not the marriage I'd envisioned. J was not acting like the husband I thought he would be for me. Hearing Trey crying from his bedroom I knew that I had to get on with my daily routine. While I would be home taking care of our son and house J would be out doing whatever with whomever. It was a realism that pushed me towards the realm of depression.

***

More and more I began to feel like J's slave instead of his wife. I took care of our son, cleaned the house, cooked his meals, and ran his errands as he instructed me to. Our monthly food allowance was $50 which I would make last as long as I could. I always wanted to make sure that my son ate above all else. At this point food was no longer important to me. I had no appetite for anything. Each day my goal was only to make it to the end of the day so that I could cry myself to sleep and pray away the anguish that consumed me.

Intimacy was a thing of the past. I couldn't bring myself to make love to a man that I knew in my spirit didn't respect or honor me anymore, never mind the fact that I was positive he was having sex with someone else. Since I wasn't giving or showing him the attention he felt that I owed to him as my husband, J began to act as though he had no reason to stay at home or be around Trey and I. He would hang out and not come home until the next day during any given day of the week. Even when he did return home it would just be to shower and grab his uniform before walking right back out of the door.

"Are you not going to at least have breakfast with your son?" I asked one morning as he was making his way to the door.

"He's barely taking solid food," J countered. "So I'd be feeding him oatmeal not having breakfast with him. You can do that."

"I can," I retorted. "But I always do. When are you going to spend some time with your son? When are you going to spend some time at *your* home with *your* family?"

It was Friday and I knew that we wouldn't see him again until Sunday night or possibly even Monday morning. I hoped that my plea would force him to see the damage he was doing to our family unit and encourage him to give us the attention we deserved. It didn't. My words were lost upon the back of his retreating figure as he carried his stuff and exited the front door without an utterance of reply.

"Why!" I screamed in frustration staring at the closed door. "Why, why, why!" I couldn't understand why it was so hard for him to love me and Trey. For him to be the husband and father that we needed him to be. I turned to walk up the hall towards the bedrooms, still ranting. "Why me?" The tears began to fall freely.

I felt myself beginning to lose control as my chest heaved with the emotional pain that had been bottled up inside of me for so long. I wanted to stop right there in the hallway and fall to the ground in surrender to the hurt but then my eyes fell upon Trey who was standing in his doorway on unsteady legs looking at me with an unmistakable sadness in his eyes. I didn't want him to see me like that so I quickly ran into the hallway bathroom, shutting and locking the door behind me. I could hear his little feet padding his way to the door and it broke my heart in pieces to know that my son was standing on the other side listening to his mother falling apart.

I cried relentlessly. *You're pitiful*, I thought. *A pitiful excuse for a mother for putting your son through this mess. At least control yourself so that he doesn't have to witness your weakness.* As I cried I looked down at my fragile, trembling hands. I was becoming afraid of my own emotional and mental stability as well as the wellbeing of both Trey and myself. J was rarely there and the money he left for me was barely sufficient for us to maintain. I needed to do something. I took a deep breath and realized that my son needed me in that moment. Despite whatever I was feeling he needed me if for nothing more than to provide him with his breakfast right then and there. I splashed cold water on my face and looked at my reflection in the mirror. I didn't like what I saw. My hair was a mess. I couldn't even remember the last time I'd combed it nicely. My face was devoid of its usual luster. Since Trey and I remained stuck in the house day in and day out I rarely gave myself a facial or applied makeup to my skin. I was becoming the pitiful women that I saw on Lifetime movies and divorce court episodes. I was no longer myself.

"Go play, Trey," I called out, knowing that he was still on the other side of the door. "Mommy's coming out to get your oatmeal." I heard him move away from the door as I continued to stare into my own eyes. "You've got to do something," I told myself. "You have got to do something."

I knew I needed to do better for my son. He was becoming the most handsome, smart, and caring little gentlemen I'd ever met. My love for him was about the only thing that got me up in the mornings. I chided myself for sometimes wondering what life would be like without Trey. I often felt that had I not gotten pregnant J and I wouldn't have gotten married and perhaps I wouldn't be living a life of misery. But, the second those thoughts entered my mind I always felt worse than before. A life without Trey just didn't make sense. I was blessed to be his mother and had to remind myself to never think of his existence in any other way. I knew that I owed it to my son to give him—us—a better life. I just needed to figure out how to do it.

I was drawing a blank. After a while the quietness from the other side of the door got my attention. Slowly, I opened the bathroom door and peeked my head out. I heard nothing, I saw nothing. I ventured out to the living room to find it empty. A bowl sat resting on the table with half eaten, lumpy oatmeal resting in it. I hurried to Trey's room, but he wasn't there either. Apparently, J had softened up and decided to actually spend some time with his son. They'd left without a word and instead of seeing this as a moment to regroup or rest, I saw it as an opportunity to escape it all.

I immediately began to walk around the house trying to figure out what I could do. Literally running away would do no good, he'd only find me. Plus, there was no way that I could leave that house knowing that he still had possession of my son. I couldn't live a life without Trey, it simply wasn't possible. The only other option that I could come up with was running away figuratively—ending it all in a manner that would have my family step up and claim rights to Trey so that way I'd know he'd be okay. I became frantic as I rummaged through the house like a mad woman trying to come in contact with anything at all that could terminate the pain that was searing through my spirit. We didn't own a gun, so that was out. As I went through the kitchen my hand lingered on the cutting board and I considered stabbing myself right in the heart that had been broken beyond repair. The reality was that I didn't have the nerve to do something so ruthless, so brutal and fatal to myself. There had to be another option.

Back in my bathroom, I raided the medicine cabinet. Razors, shaving cream, oxycodone for an injury J had sustained previously, and some Aleve that I frequently took for cramps and minor aches. I stared at the bottles and realized that my answer was right there. Taking the childproof cap off of the oxycodone I was pissed to see that there were only three pills left. It didn't matter. I figured that coupling them with the practically full bottle of Aleve would get the job done. Without giving it any more thought, I turned on the faucet, threw the three pain killers in my mouth, and then cupped some water to wash them down. I followed this routine about five more times taking as many Aleve pills as I could each time. I must have digested nearly a hundred of them and the bottle was empty by the time I turned the water off.

I closed the medicine cabinet door and stared at my reflection in the mirror. Maybe it wasn't the best way to go, but it was the only course of action that I could come up with. I envisioned people calling me a coward in the wake of my death, wondering what could possibly have been so wrong in my life that I'd make such a desperate move. If only they knew the hell that I endured on earth, then there'd be no question as to why I wanted to speed up my expiration date. I was at my wits' end and despite what anyone would have to say about it, I was now deciding that the game was over.

At peace with my decision and knowing that these would be my last few hours breathing, I turned away from my image, turned the light off, and exited the bathroom. I was beginning to feel a little lightheaded already as I climbed onto the bed that I shared with a man who no longer loved me the way I once thought he had. I laid in the middle of the mattress with my arms outstretched, staring up at the ceiling. I wondered how long it would take before I finally drifted off into an induced sleep. I imagined the look on J's face when he walked in and realized that I wasn't really sleeping, but that I was dead. Would he feel sad? Would he be remorseful? Would he blame himself? Would he care at all? I tried not to think about the effect it would have on Trey. I knew he'd never understand, especially as a child. But, child or not, even when he was grown with children of his own he probably would never realize that I did this so that he may have a chance at a better life—a life where he didn't have to stand by and watch his mother be treated like a punching bag, a doormat, or a blowup doll.

Eventually, sleep consumed me and I was out cold. I'm not sure when they came home or how long I was allowed to lay there in peaceful, drug laden slumber, but when my eyes fluttered and were greeted by the shine of the day light peeping in through my blinds, I wanted to die for sure. Regretfully, I moaned and rolled over to punch the pillows beside me. *How'd I mess this up*, I questioned myself. I couldn't even kill myself right! My plan to pass away in my sleep was completely shot to hell as the sounds of cartoons blaring from up front jarred me back to reality. I was alive. I'd never been more disappointed to wake up in my entire life. As I pulled myself upright I began to wish that I'd had more guts. *I should have just stabbed myself*, I thought. *Or cut my wrists until I sliced my veins so that I could bleed to death.* Anything would have been better than waking up to find evidence of my failed suicide attempt. Depression sunk into my spirit on a far deeper level than before.

I slid from the bed and drug myself to the bathroom. It was a struggle for me to avoid my reflection in the mirror as I busied about brushing my teeth and washing my face. I felt horrible. My stomach was doing somersaults and all I wanted to do was return to bed and hide under the covers. But, I knew that J would never leave me alone long enough to wallow in my own self-pity. As I replaced my toothbrush into the holder, the instant need to vomit took over. My body lurched forward and I barely made it to the toilet before I began to expel the contents of my stomach. My clothes, the seat of the commode, and the floor right in front of it were all soiled with nothing but yellow liquid—stomach acid. I wasn't even puking up the worthless pills that I'd downed.

Bang, bang, bang.

"Aye, you need to see about Trey, I gotta go!" J called out.

I couldn't respond to him because I was far too busy gripping the side of the toilet and trying not to throw up the organs that rested inside of me.

Bang, bang, bang.

He continued to beat on the door with a sense of urgency. Each thud against the oak seemed to be in sync with my body as I heaved again and again. There seemed to be no end to the disgusting liquid that continued to spew from my mouth. I wanted to cry. Not only had I failed to end my life, I'd also gone from being emotionally pained to physically sick. Life just wasn't fair.

"Aight, I'm leaving," J loudly informed me. "Get ya ass out of the mirror and come see about your kid. I'll be back."

I was glad to hear that he was leaving. The last thing I wanted to do was see his face or continue to hear his voice. It was because of him that I was in this pathetic position in the first place. I couldn't stand the weakling of a woman that I'd become as a result of being married to this man. For an hour I was glued to the toilet, throwing up and crying, crying and throwing up. When it finally felt as if my body was offering me some mercy, I rose from the ground and looked down at myself in disgust. I showered, brushed my teeth and washed my face again, and then left the bathroom to put on fresh clothes. My movements were slow and I felt empty yet my stomach ached. I was miserable in more ways than one. Entering the living room, I found Trey positioned in front of the television watching one of his favorite shows with a look of fear frozen on his face. If I didn't feel like crap before I definitely did then.

I assumed that he'd heard me in the bathroom throwing up relentlessly. It wasn't really something that I could discuss with him so I elected to remain silent instead. I laid down on the sofa and exhaled as Trey repositioned himself next to me. He was my solace, my only source of happiness. I couldn't help but to feel as though I was repeatedly failing him and myself. I should have been energetic and enthused about life and parenting but the truth was that I was filled with remorse and suicidal thoughts. I was in a dangerous position in life and had no clue how to climb out of the hole I'd dug for myself.

***

One night he came home from being out for several days. I heard him stumbling through the house in a drunken state. I'd been asleep with Trey but the moment I heard J enter the house intoxicated I jumped out of the bed and locked the bedroom door. I didn't want him bothering us. As he came closer to the bedroom door I got scared. I didn't know what to expect from him in this condition. Standing there trembling in my nightgown, it did not feel like it was my husband stumbling through my house. It felt more like there was an actual intruder—a stranger—in my home. I heard him attempt to turn the knob and his frustration became apparent immediately. He banged several times causing me to look over at Trey quickly to see if he had been awakened.

"Open the door!" J screamed in slur. "Who do you think you are? Locking doors in my house! This is my house!"

I had to hold my breath so that I wouldn't laugh out loud. I wanted him to think that we were both sound asleep. I figured that would make him give up and retreat to the sofa to sleep off his alcohol.

"Open up the door!" he demanded, giving the door a swift kick yet again.

The frame shook and Trey stirred in the center of my bed.

I sighed. "Go sleep on the couch!" I called out nervously. "Me and little man already sleep."

He screamed manically while banging on the door. "Open the damn door! You better unlock my door right now! Open the door!"

His banging turned into mighty kicks. Terrified yet wanting to comfort Trey who was now whimpering in fear, I returned to the bed and got under the covers. I held Trey tightly and stared at the door as J continued to kick and scream. Before I knew it he'd managed to kick the door in, splitting the frame in several places. My mouth fell open as his large silhouette entered the dimly lit bedroom.

"Please," I begged as his eyes focused in on me. "Please don't do anything to me. Our son is here in the bed with me."

J crossed the room to the bed with fury in his eyes.

My heart was pounding and my grip around Trey grew tighter. I shook my head from side to side. "Don't do this to me!" I screamed out of fear. "Don't do this to us."

"Take Trey to his room," J seethed as he stood by my side of the bed.

I shook my head, not wanting to comply with his wishes.

"Take him and put him in his bed right now!" his voice boomed loudly.

I could feel Trey trembling within my embrace. I weighed my options. I didn't want him to see whatever was about to happen and I needed to assure that he was safe. With that in mind, I crawled off of the bed on the other side, picked up Trey, and carried him to his room. I was a ball of nerves as I placed him in his bed. His eyes looked up at me frightfully and I forced a smile. "Go to sleep, baby," I told him. "It's okay. Go to sleep." I wondered if he believed me any more than I believed myself.

I lingered for a moment wondering if now would be a good time to just scoop Trey up and make a run for it. Keeping my son in this environment didn't seem like the responsible thing to do. Before I could get my thoughts together, J was standing right there beside me staring me in my face with his alcoholic breath. I wanted to scream and cry so bad but I had to suck it up long enough to make my way out of Trey's room. J trailed me out and down the hall to our bedroom. During the short and frantic march, I prayed that the Lord would swoop down and remove me from the situation that lay ahead. I was tired and weak. He was already a strong guy and with the alcohol he consumed he was like a life sized HULK as he moved behind me with his chest poked out and huffing. I was no match for him. I knew without a doubt that given all of the horrible things he'd already done to taint our marriage—tonight would be the icing on the cake.

I guess I wasn't moving fast enough for him because without warning and in the middle of my mental prayer, J pushed me across the threshold of our bedroom. As I felt onto the floor he grabbed me by my hair and threw me onto the bed. My heart thudded so loudly that it served as the soundtrack to the horrific scene playing out. I feared that my own husband was about to brutally rape me. Tears wasted no time in spilling from my eyes and running down the sides of my face only to drain into my ears. The person who once loved me was now treating me like I wasn't worth two cents. The person who used to make gentle love to me was now just trying to use my body to get rid of his frustration with life. How could this be? How could this happen to me? I gave up the world, my entire life, to be with this man and this was the thanks that I got for it.

He tore off my nightgown in one powerful rip with his mighty hand as I whimpered my plea. "Stop, please. Please don't do this." My hands seemed useless as I tried to push at his arms to pry him away from me. "Please don't!" I didn't want him to touch me, especially not in this manner. I knew that he was sleeping with other women. The thought of him being intimate with me made bile rise into my throat. "No!" I cried as I choked on it.

He pinned me down to the bed with the force of one arm as he struggled to free himself of his pants. His grunts filled my ears and I closed my eyes not wanting to watch as he violated me. I felt him move about, his weight crushing my body. The moment I felt his free hand force my legs apart my found my voice once more.

"Please," I said in a frail voice. "Use a…use a condom." I slapped at his arm as I realized he was ignoring me. "Use a condom!" I cried out. I was afraid of catching an STD from the man who had once been the love of my life. I kicked my legs as best I could as I continued to struggle underneath him.

Frustrated with my crying and resistance, J did the one thing he had yet to do which solidified the end of our love instantaneously. He punched me so hard in my face that I fell off of the edge of the bed, partially falling onto the glass nightstand. My hand smashed the glass leaving a cut that squirted blood onto my naked body and the bed covers that had tussled to the floor with me. Feeling the sting of the cut, I rushed about to get my nightgown he ripped from my body which was lying on the floor. Hysterically, I wrapped it around my hand as fast as I could to stop the bleeding. I ignored the throbbing of my face from the blow he'd given me as I watched the blood soak straight through my gown. The cut was apparently deeper than I thought.

"I need stitches," I told him in a raspy voice as he stood looking down at me in awe. "The bleeding would not stop. I need to go to the hospital." I eyed him cautiously as I rose from the floor and backed my way towards our bathroom. Hurriedly, I retrieved a bath towel and wrapped it around my hand. It didn't take long for the blood to make its way through the towel as well.

"I need to go to the hospital," I told him again, this time in a whisper as I stood in the middle of our bedroom naked, beaten, and bleeding."

J said nothing.

I sighed and headed for the closet to get some clothes. "I'll take myself," I told him.

"No!" he barked.

"I'm bleeding profusely!" I screamed. "If you're not going to take me I have to take myself."

As I began to dress I watched J snatch open the top drawer where I kept important documents. He took my passport and Visa. Then he grabbed my wallet out of my purse which was sitting on the dresser and relieved me of my credit cards and cell phone. “Go,” he told me. “But you’ll have nothing if you tell them—” his words trailed off but his threat was clear. He’d just relieved me of my entire identity and any form of getting help to leave him.

I was afraid but I had to get my hand seen about. At the emergency room they asked me what happened to my hand. Remembering J’s threat I told them that I had tripped with a glass in my hand. The nurse and doctor seemed to accept the story and within two hours’ time they gave me four stitches, wrapped my hand up nicely, and sent me on my way. By the time I exited the hospital doors the only thing that was running through my mind was how I could get away from the madness that had become my life. I couldn’t live this way anymore. After the physical abuse I’d just experienced there was no way that my life would prosper by remaining in this marriage. I was suffering and so was Trey. It just wasn’t right. But the reality of it was that I had nowhere to go and no one to turn to. I was stuck. I didn’t know anyone. I had no phone so I couldn’t call my mother. I couldn’t even send a letter because he took all my credit cards and money, leaving me with no financial freedom. I didn't want to go back to the house, but my little man was there. There was no way that I could risk running away and leaving Trey with the demon of a man I called my husband. Reluctantly, I went back home to find J laid out on the floor snoring like a bear. I tiptoed around him, entered Trey's room to pick him up out of bed, and then got into my own bed with my son deep within my embrace. I looked at Trey's sleeping figure and started to pray. I prayed to God to deliver us from the hell we'd been confined to.

"I'm not going anywhere without you," I whispered into Trey's ear. "I promise you that I'll always be with you."

The next night J stayed out again. Before he left, he grabbed a bunch of clothes which let me know that he wasn't going to return home any time soon. The moment he left I tore through his drawers in search of my documents and credit cards. My search came up with nothing and I was furious to know that he was practically holding me hostage in this marriage and in this house. Trying to find some silver lining, I had to admit that I was temporarily relieved to have a break from his domineering presence. As such, Trey and I went over to the neighbors' house for a change of scenery. The Rodríguezes' were having a small get together which Amelia had called and invited us to the day before. I figured that getting out of the house would help to take my thought off of my miserable life.

As usual, Amelia was very welcoming and inviting. She and her husband treated us very warmly like family. She gave me a long nice hug the moment we entered the house as if she knew what was going on in my life. The close contact and the sincerity of the gesture caused me to start crying. I simply could not hold back my tears at all.

Amelia pulled away and looked at me confusedly. "What's wrong?" she asked as she studied my face. Quickly, she took Trey out of my arms and motioned over towards the sofa. "Go, go! Have a seat."

I lagged over the sofa and plopped down on the edge. "I can't take it anymore," I sobbed. "I just can't do it." That was all I was able to say. My body was weary and my soul was in distress. There was no other way I could explain what I was feeling.

Amelia rocked Trey in her arms and took a seat beside me. She didn't force me to explain myself or to speak further. She simply held my son while patting my back at the same time.

Enrique came down the stairs and took one look at my distraught disposition. "Damn," he said shaking his head. He walked over and perched onto the arm of the sofa next to me. He placed his arm around my shoulders and gave his wife a knowing look. "Baby girl, we know all about it," he said in a sympathetic tone.

I looked at Amelia and then up at Enrique. I was in shook, wondering if they actually knew the details of the horrid secret I'd been harboring. "About what?" I asked meekly.

Enrique took a deep breath and looked over to Amelia once more as if asking for permission to speak.

"About what?" I asked again with desperation in my tone.

"I see him every day leaving in his truck but does not return," Enrique stated. "I work with your husband…well, actually he is my boss so there is nothing I can comfortable say to him. He outranks me. But one thing I know…you definitely don't deserve that. Even when you guys came over on Christmas and he stayed away for two hours. Who does that?"

I lowered my head, ashamed to know that even my neighbors knew that my husband was constantly cheating on me.

"If you want to you can stay over our house tonight," Amelia offered. "If you want to—"

I looked at her and felt like a helpless child. "I just wanted some comfort...a break from being stuck in the house all day and night. I don't feel safe in my house. He might come home drunk again." I thought about the way he had attacked me and looked down at my bandaged arm. Suddenly I longed for my mother.

"Do you have family here?" Amelia asked me as if reading my thoughts.

"In the states yes, but they are in Georgia…my sisters. My mom is all the way in Germany."

She smiled at me warmly. “You know you can call long distance with our phone.”

The opportunity was divine. I wanted to call my mom so bad but then I knew that she would be worried and want me to come back home. I couldn’t tell her that J had taken all of my paperwork with him. She would have a heart attack if she knew the truth about what was going on. Wanting to spare my mother the heartbreak, I declined the offer to call her. I did however accept the Rodríguezes’ offer to spend the night. It was the most peaceful rest I’d gotten in months and when I awoke in the morning I felt so rejuvenated that I allowed Amelia to talk me into calling my mother anyway.

Germany they were nine hours ahead so I was surprised that she was still up since it was 11:30 PM over there.

“What’s wrong my child?” my mother asked the moment she answered the phone. “I have not heard from you and now you call so I know something is going on.” There is a saying that if you don’t hear from your kids they are fine, but you should get worried once you hear from them.

"It's nothing," I told her. "J and I have had a couple of arguments here and there but…we're okay." My voice quivered as I tried to convince her that things were fine.

"Stop lying. I can hear it in your voice."

I didn't have the strength to argue with her.

"What number are you calling from?" she asked pensively. "Is it a number that I can call back if I need to speak to you?"

"Umm, hold on," I told her. I looked to Amelia. "Is it okay if my mom calls here every now and then to check on us?"

Amelia was placing fresh linen on the guest bed while watching Trey tear up a Nutrigrain bar she'd just given him. "Of course," she told me.

I mouthed thank you and returned to my call. "Yes, Ma. You can call this number back," I told her.

"Melissa," my mother called my name lovingly. "My child, you know you can always come back home."

I felt myself getting choked up and I had to move the phone away from my face so that she wouldn't hear me as I started crying. I wanted to go home so bad. "I love you, Mama," I told her.

"I love you too."

Hanging up that phone was the hardest thing for me to do.

***

Shortly after my getaway at the Rodríguezes' J received orders to be transferred to Killeen, Texas with only a three-week notice. I found that strange but didn't dare question it.

"You need to start packing," he'd said upon coming home from work one day. "I'm being transferred to Texas."

I stood in front of the stove where I was preparing dinner and turned to face him. "What do you mean by *you're* being transferred?" I asked. "It's all of us that have to go." I was saddened by the idea of moving to another place where I knew no one. At least here I had the Rodríguezes that I could turn to in case of an emergency.

"You're not coming," he said sternly. "I'm taking Trey with me, but not you."

I was livid. It was one thing to beat on me and cheat on me, but it was another thing to talk about taking my child away from me. I pointed my wooden spatula at him and narrowed my eyes. "I am still your wife," I hissed. "And if you're leaving and wanting my son to go then we're all leaving. But there's no way in hell that I'm letting you take Trey without me!"

He plopped down into a chair at the kitchen table with a beer in his hand unfazed by my irate response. "The military's only paying for me to travel over so I can't take you with me, Melissa."

I knew better than to believe the lie he was feeding me. I'd grown up around military professionals all my life so he was going to have to try to fool someone else with his lies.

"Look, the fact is that we're getting a divorce," he said, as realizing that his lie wasn't going to cut it.

The word divorce sounded like music to my ears. I was sure that it was the best thing to do because obviously our marriage wasn't working out. I desperately need to get away from him and lately doing so wasn't easy. But, now that he'd decided it was time for us to sever ties, I had the out I'd been looking for. Just as I began to release a sigh of relief he hit me with something else.

"Until that actually happens we keeping everything the way it is," he told me.

My eyes fluttered with confusion. "And that means?"

He gave me a sinister smile as he rose from the table. "You'll see," he told me.

I was petrified of what hellish plan he had in store for me.

Over the next few weeks I packed all of our belongings and sadly said goodbye to the Rodríguezes'. Amelia had begged me to stay but I couldn't let J take my son away and he was still holding all of my important paperwork hostage. On the way to Texas we stopped off in Louisiana.

Apparently J had taken some vacation time before starting at his new post and decided that he wanted to visit his family—the same family that he often lied about saying that they were from Puerto Rico. I'd known when he received the call from Louisiana while we were in Atlanta on vacation that his family hailed from no parts of Puerto Rico. Once I actually met his parents I learned that they were both born and raised right there in Louisiana. I couldn't believe the extent of J's lies.

The experience of meeting J's family was great for Trey since he'd never had a chance to socialize with that side of his lineage. He enjoyed himself to the fullest as he played all day long with his new found cousins. I was happy for little man. But, while Trey was getting to know his family, his father spent his days hanging out and drinking with God knows who.

"You and little man have to stay here in Louisiana while I go get everything situated in Texas," he informed me as he returned home. "It's going to take a couple of days to get a house and for the furniture to arrive."

I was livid for a moment. It was my understanding that he'd already made all of those arrangements. But as he drunkenly fell into bed I realized that maybe this was a blessing in disguise. "Okay," I told him, wondering if finally, I'd be able to somehow break free. "That's fine."

I watched his head fall back against the covers as he began to snore loudly. He hadn't even heard my sarcasm. I crossed my arms and stared at him praying that it was the last time I'd ever have to see him.

~ Chapter 5~

Autoimmune Hepatitis

"The part can never be well unless the whole is well." –Plato

In J's absence, I got to know his family better and my son had lots of fun enjoying his cousins. It felt good to see him laughing and playing around other children. It felt even better to feel that we were in a safe environment. My father-in-law, Robert, had the most space so we stayed with him. He made sure that Trey and I were comfortable. Just days after J left for Texas my mother-in-law, Christine, invited us out for dinner to a Chinese buffet. I was so excited because with the strict budget J had us on we hadn't had Chinese food in a while. I ate, or at least tried out anything that they had to offer. I couldn't remember the last time that I'd eaten so much and so freely. My eyes saw the myriad of options and my stomach wanted to try it all. But, on the way back to the house I started to feel a little nauseated. Immediately I knew that I'd eaten too much. As soon as we returned home I had to lay down. I couldn't get any further than the couch with the way my body was feeling so I crashed right there while the family tended to Trey.

The next morning when I woke up my sister-in-law, Jessie, had the great idea to go shopping.

"Yessss!" I agreed. I hadn't been shopping in so long so I was super excited. "Let me just get our stuff together."

"No, no," Jessie stated. "This is an all-girls trip, sweetie. So, get Trey and we'll drop him off to my mom."

I wasn't going to argue. I loved my son undyingly but I welcomed the opportunity to have some adult time and maybe let my hair down a little bit. So, I dressed and rode with Jessie to drop Trey off at his grandmother's house. I had no reservations about leaving him with Ms. Christine because I saw firsthand how she loved my son and was genuinely fond of him.

As I got back into the car Jessie looked at me with a ghastly expression. "Melissa, look at me," she instructed.

I turned to the left to look her in the face with my eyebrow raised. "What?"

She covered her mouth with her hand. "Oh my goodness! What is wrong with your eyes? Ugh! Jesus! You look like an alien!"

Her tone and expression were so stunning that I couldn't help but laugh. "What are you talking about, girl?"

"Your eyes are yellow!" she screamed.

I pulled down the mirror on the visor in front of me and gasped. Indeed, the inside of my eyes which were usually white were now neon yellow. I hadn't even noticed upon washing my face and pulling my hair into a ponytail. I could understand why she was alarmed but I figured that maybe it was just allergies or my eyes getting adjusted to the air in Louisiana. "Wow," I stated, staring at the yellowness. But, I shook it off and gave Jessie a reassuring smile. "But I'm fine, girl. No worries."

She didn't look so sure. "Hmmm. You need to get checked out."

"I will," I said in an uncertain tone that even I didn't believe. "But not now, girl. I'm just excited to finally get out of this little country hick town. I just wanna go have fun. Don't worry about it. It might be food poisoning, you know. I had Chinese food last night and felt bad afterwards," I rationalized. All I wanted to do was go shopping. Nothing was going to deter us from having this much needed girls' day.

Although Jessie was apprehensive about it, she put the car in drive and we were off. We stayed out and about all day. I was lucky to find some nice pieces that were inexpensive. Browsing through the selections of the shops we happened upon was therapeutic and relaxing as Jessie and I got to know one another better. I was enjoying myself but as the day began to wind down I started to feel weak. I tried to keep moving and not make a big deal out of it, but Jessie could tell by my demeanor that something was wrong.

"You ready to call it a day?" Jessie asked, watching me holding onto the rack of a row of dresses.

I gave her a weak smile. "I just…I think I need some energy. Food maybe."

So we stopped to get some fast food after leaving the mall. I thought that maybe my wooziness was because I hadn't had anything to eat all day. We settled upon McDonalds and I had a double cheeseburger meal. After I ate I was starting to feel a little better, but not for long. I didn't have the strength to go on to the nail shop that Jessie had planned to take us to for manicures. Thinking it best that she gets me home to rest, we headed back to the country where J's family resided in various areas. During the ride back to Robert's house I felt like I would pass out at any minute.

"Melissa?" I heard Jessie call out to me.

I felt like I was in and out of consciousness and I just wanted to curl up and block out the way my body was torturing me.

"Melissa?" Jessie called to me again, this time placing her hand on my shoulder.

"Hmmm," I mumbled, unable to actually speak because I was consumed with a weakness that I just couldn't explain.

"Okay, you're gonna stay with me for the night," she stated. "Dad's out of town and I don't like the idea of you staying at the house by yourself so…yeah. We'll get Trey in the morning."

I didn't argue. I felt more comfortable knowing that someone would be around just in case I took a turn for the worse. I heard Jessie pull out her cell phone and call Ms. Christine to let her know that I would pick Trey up in the morning and that I wasn't feeling well. The arrangement was fine with Ms. Christine and I immediately felt blessed to have people in my corner.

"Are you okay?" Jessie asked as we pulled up to her house. "Here, let me help you to the door." She got out of the driver's seat, helped me out of the car, and assisted me up the walk to her front door. "It's gonna be alright, honey." She helped me into the house and allowed me to lay on her bed. "Are you okay?"

I felt bad that our girls' day had ended with me getting sick. Two nights in a row now I'd been knocked out by my body creating yet another catastrophic end to what would have been a great family moment.

"You need anything, Melissa?" Jessie asked, placing a cool cloth over my forehead. "Are you okay?"

I wasn't really feeling like I was well at all but I didn't want to worry anyone or put Jessie out any more than I already had. I nodded my head slowly. "I'm okay. I'll be fine."

She left me alone to rest and I willed myself to fall asleep. But, every time I closed my eyes I was scared that they wouldn't open back up. I didn't know what was overcoming me, but fear filled my spirit. Soon after Jessie left me shortness of breath kicked in. I found myself gasping in the darkness, trying to get my lungs to refill with oxygen but it just didn't' seem to be enough. Panic replaced fear and I struggled to sit up against the pillows on the bed. I removed the cool cloth Jessie had given me which had now turned warm. I clutched at my chest as it heaved in response to my continuous struggle for air. I was scared to go to sleep. Something was wrong.

For hours I sat in the dark, afraid of what was happening to me. It was almost midnight and I still could not sleep. Unsure of what the matter was and in need of some kind of comfort, I decided to call my husband. I hadn't heard from him since the day that he'd left for Texas. To my dismay I received no answer all three times that I dialed his number. With no other recourse, I left him a voice message after the third call to let him know that I wasn't feeling too well. I put the phone down and said a small prayer. "Jesus, please be with me. Whatever this is, please be with me." I felt the tears welling up but didn't want to grant them access to fall. I didn't need to get all emotionally worked up at a time when I was already struggling to breathe. So I stared at the ceiling, grasping handfuls of the blanket tightly, and counted until I eventually drifted off into an uncomfortable slumber.

I didn't hear back from J until the next day. He called early that morning as I was trying to pull myself together to go and get Trey.

"I'm coming to get y'all," he announced, sounding more country than I'd ever heard him sound.

"What?" I questioned, not understanding what was happening and feeling a tad light headed falling my trying night.

"I'm on my way back to get you and Trey," he explained. "I got a nice two-bedroom house in a safe area so you should like it."

My heart fluttered. His words almost made me feel like he did still care about his family. I was glad to hear that, especially when I felt like I really needed him right now given how sick I'd been over the past couple of days. "That's great, J" I told him.

"Yeah, so I'll be there sometime this evening so make sure you have y'all stuff together."

I wasn't excited about the task of packing up the few things that Trey and I had been left with, but I was actually kind of looking forward to J's arrival. Perhaps this was going to be a new beginning for our family. We'd vowed to love one another through sickness and in health, for better or for worse. We'd seen what I felt was the worse any relationship could come to. I couldn't deny that I loved my husband and the truth was that no one had ever said that marriage was easy. I hoped that once I was well again and we were settled into our new home that we would find our way back to loving each other the way marriage was designed to encompass love. During our phone call I didn't mention again how bad I was feeling. He was in such good spirits about the home he'd secured that I didn't want to upset him and bring down the mood. For the greater good of keeping the peace and holding on to my tiny bit of joy over finally going home, I just decided to keep my mouth shut. Besides, whatever was ailing me was sure to subside soon.

***

Upon his arrival J didn't even realize that my eyes were still that same icky neon yellow tint. He greeted his family, roughhoused with Trey, but never paid close attention to his wife. Feeling as if he wasn't concerned about me I finally approached him and turned his face towards mine so that he couldn't help but notice that something was wrong. "Look at me," I told him.

His left eyebrow rose. “I see you.”

“No, no. Look at me. Look at my eyes. They are yellow! I think I’m sick or something.”

He lightly removed my hands from his face. “Sure you’re sick,” he said in a joking manner. “Sick in the head.” He laughed at his own condescending joke.

Here I was being serious and he wanted to insult me. The only reason I felt compelled to speak on it was because despite my mind over matter mentality during the course of the day, my body just wouldn’t seem to cooperate. The fact that he was so uncaring about my issue made me want to cry. I wondered what had changed since he left Texas earlier that morning because then he was kind and seemed to care for and miss his family. It was clear that he was now back to being the insensitive J that I was used to.

I shook my head. “Wow!” I exclaimed while walking away.

"What you shaking your head for?" he snapped. "Stop stuffing everything in your mouth and you'll probably have regular eyes then."

I took a seat on the sofa, feeling myself becoming overexerted and frustrated. *Something is really wrong with this dude*, I thought. I really didn't understand how his brain worked sometimes. "You're the one sick in the head to make a statement like that to me," I told him, unable to keep my emotions in check.

He sucked his teeth. "There you go getting on my nerves already. You better chill out, little girl."

Little girl? I couldn't believe his nerve. *Here we go*, I thought. *Nothing has changed.* "Get yourself together cause I'm not up for dealing with your attitude all the way to Texas," he said. "I'm tired too so we're staying here another day before heading back."

I gave him a surprised look. He'd made it clear that I needed to have myself and Trey ready to go when he got here and now here he was saying that we had another day before leaving. I could have been resting the whole time I was busting my butt getting our belongings together. But I said nothing. I didn't have the strength or the desire to argue with J. That night we slept separately and when morning came my energy level was no higher than it was the days prior.

"Look, wherever you go today, like hanging out with your family, please take your son with you," I told J as he got dressed for the day. "I'm not able to take care of him today. I need to rest."

"Lil man's going to be just fine," he responded nonchalantly.

Uggghhh! I knew that meant that he was going to leave Trey there with me and his mother, whose house we'd stayed at overnight. True to form, J left without taking Trey. All day I stayed in the house because it was far too hot to go outside. Trey and I camped out on the couch in front of the television. By the time evening came I was adamant about not spending another night on Ms. Christine's couch. She was a gracious hostess but her home was filled with too many people and there simply wasn't enough room for another family. J had yet to reappear and I desperately needed to get sufficient rest before we got on the road for Texas. Biting the bullet, I called my father-in-law in hopes that he wasn't busy.

"Hello?" he answered the phone jovially.

"Hey Mr. Robert, it's Melissa," I announced myself. "I was wondering if you wouldn't mind picking up me and Trey and bringing us back to the house."

"Hmmm…where's J?" he inquired.

I was afraid that I was about to be denied my request. "I'm not sure but he hasn't come back. And I--"

"Say no more," he interjected. "I'm on my way."

It took less than an hour for Robert to show up and then transport us back to his home. I was very appreciative of him as well as the space his home allotted us. After bathing Trey and putting him in the guest bed for the night, I tried to enjoy a relaxing bath but my body wouldn't relax at all. Later on that night J came over to his dad's house to check on our son. He stormed through the door with an attitude alarming me yet Trey didn't stir.

"What's wrong with you?" I hissed.

He ignored my question and tried to wake Trey up.

"Leave him alone," I insisted. "Why would you want to wake him up?"

J looked at me and spoke vehemently. "Shut up!" I could smell the liquor on is breath and I knew that it was going to be a long night.

"Look," I spoke calmly, hoping to redirect his attitude. "Just let Trey rest and you go on and get you some sleep too, okay?"

Instead of him just walking back out of the door and taking my advice, he rounded the bed to my side and placed his face right in front of mine. "Why on God's green earth are you talking to me?"

I was nervous that in his intoxicated demeanor he would do something dreadful with my son laying right beside me, but I silently prayed that he would find the good sense to back off. "I just don't want you to wake up our son. What's wrong with that?"

He failed to respond. He simply gave me a blank look as if he was having difficulty processing what I'd said.

"Look, just forget about it and leave please," I said softly. "It's okay…it's all good. Just…just go to bed."

His next question stung and immediately I wanted to spit in his face. "Why do you look so ugly today?"

"Dude, I am sick!" I shot back. "I am not feeling well or did you forget? I don't know what you expect out of me. You don't even care that I am sick so why don't you just leave us alone and let us sleep in peace!"

He started cursing and calling me every name in the book. Trey began to awaken from the ruckus that his father was keeping up and I was becoming livid with the insults that J kept hurling my way.

"You ugly winch!" he hollered as spit from his mouth landed on the tip of my nose. "You're so disgusting I don't see how any man could ever wanna bone you. Stupid bitch! You're nothing, Melissa! An ugly sack of nothing!"

"Shut up!" I screamed at J as Trey began to cry. "Shut up, shut up, shut—"

BAM! In midsentence J hauled off and punched me dead in the face. Immediately my hands flew up to my nose and I could feel the blood spilling into my palms.

"What did you did that for you bully?" I cried out. Not knowing how far his aggression was going to propel his violence, I jumped up to go get a towel from the hallway bathroom.

As I hurried up the hall, J's stepmom, Tina, came running out of her bedroom. She took one glance the blood dripping through my fingers as I moved swiftly past her and then back at J who was huffing about in pursuit of me. "I know you did not just hit her!" she screamed out, putting two and two together.

Tina worked nights and I had been sure that she was taking her daily nap. It was just my luck that that night it was her day off. She'd obviously heard our altercation and had come out into the hall to see what was going on.

As I held a towel to my face, J brushed past me and headed for the door with the short and fiery Tina upon his heels.

"Get out of my house you demon!" Tina squealed. "Get out! Who are you? Who taught you that it was okay to go around putting your hands on women? I can't believe that you hit her you punk! That's your wife!"

J didn't bother to turn around to address her ranting. He simply walked out of the door and slammed it behind him.

Tina turned to me in fright. "Oh my god." She walked over to me and embraced me in her arms.

From down the hall I could hear Trey crying and I wanted to simply fall through the floor. My life was in shambles.

"Was that the first time, Melissa?" Tina asked, pulling back from our embrace to look me in the eyes. "Or is this a common thing?" Her eyes were filled with concern.

I couldn't lie to her. I was tired of covering up the abusive nature of my marriage, pretending that everything was okay when I was slowly dying inside. "No, it has happened before," I admitted.

Trey's wails grew louder.

"I have to go see about Trey," I announced sniffing back sobs.

"I got it," Tina offered.

I followed her back to the guest room and watched helplessly as she picked him up and started to walk him around the house until he fell back asleep. Once he was at peace, she returned him to his comfortable position in the bed and she and I retreated to the living room where we sat on the sofa and she examined my face.

"How many times has he done that to you?" she asked me.

I looked away from her stare. "He does it all the time. I don't know why."

She shook her head in disbelief. "No way. Why in the world are you still with him?"

It was a good question for which I didn't have an answer. "I don't know," I admitted. "I do it for my son. We have nowhere to go."

"But Melissa, you not doing Trey any good like this, honey. Do you think he wants to grow up to see his mom getting abused by his dad? Don't no child want to see that. I know it's easier said than done but this is not healthy for you or your son."

"I know." My heart was aching. "What other options do I have though? I gave up everything for this man. I don't have anything to go back to. You know I came from overseas. All my family in the United States is in Atlanta. I know that I have to figure something out but…I don't know what. He took all my documents. I have nothing."

"Melissa, look at me," Tina said. The tone of her voice had changed from cautionary to concerned.

I looked at her and noticed the horror in her eyes. "What is it? Is my face swollen or something?"

She shook her head. "No…no…but umm…seriously, what's wrong with your eyes?"

"I don't know," I shrugged, realizing that she was noticing my yellow sclera in both of my eyes. "I haven't been feeling so well. I been nauseated all day. A couple of nights ago after dinner I was feeling bad. I think I got food poisoning."

"We all had that food, Melissa. There was nothing wrong with the food. The place was very clean and they use fresh products. That can't be what it is. Besides, it's been days since then and like I said, the rest of us didn't get sick from the food. Now, I'm an RN and I know that there is something else going on here. It looks more like you have jaundice..." She studied me intently. "Open your mouth."

I followed instructions and she took a look inside of my mouth.

"Oh God!" she exclaimed. "Goodness. Everything is yellow. Your eyes, the inside of your mouth…Let me take a look at your hands." She grabbed my hands and inspected my skin thoroughly. "Yes Melissa. Baby, you have to go to the hospital. You're yellow everywhere. We gotta do something. Call J." She hesitated, considering what she'd just said. "Oh never mind. All that alcohol he had, forget him. I'm just going to go ahead and drive you myself." Tina was up and on the move.

"Wait! Where are we going and what's going to happen to my son?" I was nervous. If something was truly wrong with me I feared that I would be taken away from Trey for a while.

Tina turned back to look at me. "No matter what, of course I will take care of him. You don't have to worry about him. We gotta take care of you."

I began to tremble. "I'm scared. I don't want to go."

"You have to go. We don't know what's wrong with you and somebody needs to find out. This is something serious. Now get dressed," she added with finality.

In no time, she and I were headed to the hospital with a drowsy Trey in the backseat. Tina felt obligated to let my deadbeat of a husband know what was going on so she continued to try to reach him by phone.

"J, we're going to the hospital," she said to his voice mail. "Something's wrong with Melissa. I need you to meet us there to pick up Trey so I can stay with Melissa. Whatever you're doing, get yourself down there to the hospital." Dissatisfied with having to leave a message, Tina called Ms. Christine's house and was equally as pissed to receive no answer.

At the emergency room, the doctor on duty didn't really know what to do with me. The whole time he examined me he just kept looking at me in awe stating that I was indeed very sick.

"We're going to need to consult with a specialist," Dr. Adams told me. "Our facility is very small and there just isn't anyone available with umm…the expertise we need right now who can uh…really…really take a look at you." My face must have told the story of my trepidation because he immediately changed his tone. "But, let's get some blood tests done for now and once the results come back we can get back with you."

Was he sending me away? "Dr. Adams, please," I begged. Now that Tina had pulled me down to the hospital despite my fears I didn't want to leave without any answers. "Can you tell me *something*?

Anything? Please. I'm scared and I can't leave not knowing anything."

Dr. Adams took a deep breath. "I'll be honest with you. In examining you I know that there's a whole lot going on here…a lot that we're just not equipped to diagnosis or handle given our limitations here. To better serve you we'd need to transfer you to a bigger hospital. At best, we can run these tests, send them to an outside lab, and get them assessed. I can expedite it and after that I can call you tomorrow with your results. Okay?"

No, it wasn't okay. "But Dr. —"

"Again Ma'am, this hospital is only for small emergencies. We simply cannot help you here beyond what I've already offered to do."

I sighed heavily. "So I guess I'm going back home," I said in a defeated manner.

"Yes, ma'am. For now."

As I walked out of the room I found my stepmother was waiting for me patiently in the tiny waiting room. I could see the question in her eyes as I exited through the small doors empty handed with a frown upon my lips.

"They can't help me," I told her. "They said there was nothing they could do because they weren't equipped to deal with my issue."

"That's insane!" Tina exclaimed.

"It's okay," I said waving her off. "We are heading back to Texas in the morning so maybe I'll be able to see someone there."

Reluctantly we returned home and I crawled into bed with Trey once again. J never bothered to return his stepmother's call during the entire ordeal. I felt helpless and longed for home. For the rest of the night I couldn't sleep. I kept on wondering what could possibly be wrong with me. Before I knew it the sun was up and a new day had begun. It was morning. I got Trey and I dressed and Tina graciously drove us over to Ms. Christine's so that we head out on our way to Texas. Once we got there I knocked on the door several times and received no answer. Everyone must have been asleep. I continued to knock and five minutes later J opened the door.

He squinted to look at us and I felt that he looked a whole lot worse than I felt. All he had on was his basketball shorts with no shirt. "What you want?" he snarled, acting as if he wasn't going to let us in.

"What you mean what I want? You said we was leaving today. How come you not dressed? I'm ready to go."

He looked at me and shook his head. "No, we not leaving today. I had way too much to drink last night."

I was exasperated. I was looking forward to moving on so that I could get some medical attention outside of the country town he had us currently staying in. "I need to see a doctor A.S.A.P," I told him. "I was at the ER last night but they couldn't help me."

J huffed and walked away, leaving the door wide open. "Man, you gonna' be okay. When were you at the ER yesterday?"

I entered the house and led Trey into the living room where J fell onto the couch. "Last night. Your stepmom was calling you and you didn't answer the phone." I turned the television on the Disney channel to occupy Trey. "Look," I said sitting on the edge of the sofa next to J. "I'm very sick."

"Mmmhmm," J responded with his eyes closed. "Sick in the head." That response wasn't funny the first time he said it and it wasn't funny this time either.

Trey began to whine. "Jue, Ma-Ma. Jue." He wanted his juice.

"I don't know what y'all gonna do now because y'all can't stay here," J snapped displaying his annoyance. "There's no room and everyone is still sleep."

"Are you kidding me now?" Was he really about to put his wife and kid out?

"How did you get over here in the first place? I thought Pop had to go out on a late trip."

"He did. Your stepmom dropped us of."

"Well then call her back to come get you."

“With what phone?” I asked since I didn’t currently have a cell phone of my own.

J reached for his. “Shit, I’ll call her.” He dialed Tina’s number and waited for her to answer. “Aye, I need you to come back and get them…naw, we not leaving ‘til tomorrow or something. There’s no room so…mannnn…Where’s Pop? He back yet? Fine…I don’t need all that so…yeah, yeah. Okay. Whatever.” He disconnected the call without saying goodbye.

I figured that Tina must have been going off on him.

“Hey Pop,” he said, having placed another call to his dad. “You back from that trip? Can you stop and get Melissa and Trey on your way home? We gotta stay put for a while.”

For a while? I wondered if he ever really intended to make the trip to Texas.

“How long? Yeah…yeah, that’s good. Thanks.” J tossed his phone onto the coffee table. “Tina’s about to go to some retreat for her job so my dad should be back from his run soon and he can scoop you and lil man. He'll be here in about an hour.

"Jue Ma-Ma! Jue!" Trey continued to beg.

I rose from the sofa to retrieve his sippy cup from his bag and then headed in the direction of the kitchen as Trey's whine turned into a wailing fit.

"Aye, you gotta get outta here with all that," J said.

"He just needs his juice."

"Outside, man!" J snapped, rising from the sofa and snatching up Trey's bag. He picked up our crying son and walked to the front door. "Folk trying to sleep in here."

"What are you doing?" I complained.

He opened the door, tossed Trey's bag onto the porch, and then sat the baby down beside it. "Y'all gotta wait out here with all that noise."

"Are you serious?" I asked, standing behind him.

"Go on. He'll be here in a minute."

How an hour dwindled down to a minute was intriguing to me. I held Trey's cup up. "Can I at least get him some juice?"

"You shoulda came prepared," J replied, snatching me by the arm and slinging me out of the door.

I stumbled over Trey's bag and my fall only made our son cry louder.

"Ugh! Don't nobody wanna hear all this. Dang!" J slammed the door in my face.

I shuttered at the reality of the moment. My toddler was whiny and my body was tired as we both sat out in the eighty-degree sun while my husband returned to his peaceful slumber. This wasn't right. I wanted to break down, bang on the door, and yell out my displeasure with J's demeaning behavior. But, my son was watching me. He'd been through enough of seeing me abused and now being put out of his grandmother's house by his father. It would do neither of us any good for me to lose control in front of him now. So, I grabbed Trey into a big bear hug, threw a plastic smile onto my face, and tickled him relentlessly. His tiny squeals of joy made all the difference in the world when I was truly dying on the inside.

It was burning up as we continued to sit outside waiting. Surprisingly, Trey remained peaceful as he played around on the porch. Every once in a while he would get up to hug me and give me kisses and then sit right back down. My love for him made everything seem a bit easier to deal with. I loved his loving and caring personality. He always knew how to make me feel better.

Two hours later Ms. Christine stepped out of the house. “Heyyyy!” she said in shock. “Why y’all sitting outside in this heat on this hot porch?”

Ha! It was a great question. “You should ask your son that,” I told her.

She frowned up and then ushered us inside. “Well, come on in, darling. It’s too hot out here for you and the baby!”

I rose from my position on the top step of her porch. “Thank you,” I said in a faint tone. The sun had nearly zapped up any energy that I’d managed to store despite whatever was ailing my body.

"What's wrong with you?" Ms. Christine asked. "Why you looking all cranky and funny?"

I sighed. "I'm sick and I need to go see a doctor but your son won't take me," I explained as Trey and I followed Ms. Christine inside. "Now we're going to be here for another day and I'm not even sure where we going to sleep at. He said Robert was coming back to get us but he hasn't showed up yet."

We all trailed into the kitchen where Ms. Christine took it upon herself to pour up some juice for Trey.

I slid down into a chair and nearly fainted. "I'm pissed so pissed, Mom!" I let out. I felt comfortable calling her that since she'd been so warm and inviting towards me.

"Why y'all left from over there anyway then if you ain't leaving today?" Once she asked me that I knew exactly where her son got his attitude from. Never mind the fact that her son had his wife and child baking in the heat. Never mind the fact that her son wouldn't take his wife to a reputable hospital be seen about.

I felt slighted by the way she snapped at me. "Because I thought we were leaving today since that's what *he* told me…Obviously that's not going to happen." I looked away from her so she wouldn't see the hurt in my yellow eyes.

"Well y'all can just stay here," she said in a softer tone. "You know we'll make some room for you guys."

I appreciated the gesture but I was really floored that she would have the audacity to speak to me as if I was some stranger off of the street. I had my hands full and on top of feeling horrible I would now be stuck in Ms. Christine's house all day where there was no room for me and my son, no air on despite the sweltering heat blazing outside, very little food for all of the occupants of the home yet alone two more guests, and a drunk husband who obviously didn't care about anything that went on with us. I wanted to cry and be anywhere other than Louisiana at that moment.

Thirty minutes later J woke up. I was still at the kitchen table, sprawled across it because I just couldn't move. I was feeling worse and worse by the minute. As J entered the kitchen and began to get himself a glass of water, I had no choice but to try to appeal to his kinder side, if one so existed within him at this time.

"J," I said softly. "Can we please leave today? I know you're tired, honey. I'm so sorry for that, but I need to see a doctor for real."

"You can wait another day," he told me. "Chill out. It ain't that serious. Quit trying to make everything about you."

As much as I was trying to fight back my tears I couldn't. They just started to roll down my face and would not stop.

He frowned at me as he gulped his water. "What the hell are you crying for now.?" he growled. "I'm so sick of you always with that bullshit. Grow up dammit you can wait another day!"

"Stop screaming at me!" I retorted. "You don't even understand how much you hurt me. I'm in physical and emotional pain. And trust me, the emotional pain is the worst."

As he walked out of the kitchen door I grabbed a dish towel off of the table and threw it at his retreating figure. He turned around and picked the towel up as it had fallen to the ground. I watched him take deliberate steps back inside of the kitchen and over to the table where I sat, all the while wringing the towel tightly. Before I could move or say a word he popped me in the face, on the head, shoulders, arms, and legs with the towel leaving whelps on my skin.

"Great, Melissa!" he barked as he continued to snap at me, despite my flailing hands. "When are you going to learn? Stupid ass!"

His inflictions didn't even hurt. I was so used to being in pain caused by him that I just didn't feel the physical aspect of it now. How could one person be so mean and cruel to his own family? As he whipped at me with the towel, his cell phone rang. He threw the towel at me and answered the call. I stared at my arms as he listened to the caller and then hung up in frustration.

"He's not coming," J spat out. "Said he can't make it over."

J was pissed but I was disappointed for a different reason. J didn't want us there but I didn't want to stay in the warm, cramped up home of his mother only to be insulted and repeatedly abused by my husband all evening and night. But, as fate would have it, I had no choice but to stay put at Ms. Christine's. Her home was filled with his brother's children that Ms. Christine had custody of. The only plus was that Trey enjoyed the time spent with his cousins. I did my best to steer clear of J for the rest of the day. It was easy to do considering he spent most of his time away from his mother's house until nightfall.

In the morning we were finally getting ready to leave. I was excited about getting out of Louisiana. Our things were already at Ms. Christine's, packed and ready to go. As soon as J finished taking his precious time loading the car we began to say our goodbyes.

"Hold up!" Ms. Christine called from down the hall as we stood on the front porch. She dragged a rolling suitcase along behind her and approached us with a smile on her face. "I'm riding with you," she announced.

Immediately, I turned to look at J but, his face was just as shocked as mine. *I know she is not thinking that she is going to stay with us*, I thought.

"I'm going stay with my sister Antty for a couple of days out in Houston," she said.

"Mom, Houston's six hours from here," J commented.

"So? You can't take your mom to visit her kin?" Ms. Christine snapped back.

J exhaled loudly and snatched up his mother's bag to add to our luggage that was stored in the trunk. I knew that our new home in Harker Heights was only a four-hour drive from where we were. The thought of us driving two hours past our destination and then another two hours back made me sick to my stomach. I needed a doctor quickly and every day it seemed as if my chances of being seen about were becoming more and more slim to none.

The commute was pretty quiet and uneventful. After dropping his mom off in Houston we ended up stuck in traffic for over four hours so we didn't get to Harker Heights until midnight. By that time, we were all cranky and tired and it was obviously too late to try to find a doctor. I didn't complain though because I didn't have the energy to fight with J. I simply prayed that I was able to make it through the night. By the time we got to our new home I didn't even care about the house. I was in no mood for a tour. All I wanted to do was go to sleep and wake up the next morning so that I could finally see a doctor who was capable of telling me what was wrong with me.

***

The next day J finally drove me to the military hospital. I waited four hours until somebody even so much as took a look at me! They did all they could, yet they still couldn't figure anything out. They ran a series of tests and after studying the results the doctor was perplexed.

"All of your test results seem normal," Dr. Sandler stated. "Ma'am, we apologize but to better serve you we're going to have to transfer you to a different hospital. I think we're just not able to help you here."

I was overcome with grief and frustration. What was so wrong with me that no one, not even army medical professionals, was able to help me? My tears wouldn't resist the urge to fall and I became unable to respond to the doctor.

"So, we're going to go ahead and transfer her to K&T hospital in Temple, Texas," Dr. Sandler told J.

"Fine," J replied in short manner. "So, you can take care of that without me right? We just moved here and we don't have anyone to watch our son so I need to head to Houston to drop him off with my mother."

The thought of Trey leaving me was too much for me to bear. "Why does he have to go with your mom? I might be out of the hospital quicker than you think. They don't even know what it is! You don't know how long I am going to be hospitalized because *they* don't even know."

J totally ignored me. "Yeah, so Dr. Sandler, I'm going to go back to the house to get my wife some clothes and I'll be back shortly."

"No problem, sir," Dr. Sandler stated.

In front of the doctor J made it seem like he was such a caring and wonderful husband. I knew the truth. He was just looking for the fastest way to get away from me.

"So you're not going to take me to the other hospital?" I asked him in disbelief.

"No, dear," he responded. "I have to go drop off little man and get you some clothes. The doctor has it under control here."

"Ah, yes," Dr. Sandler jumped in. "The paramedics will transport you from here to K&T."

"See," J said, giving me a menacing smirk. "I'll see you over there." He patted my head like I was a puppy and made a beeline for the exit with Trey in tow.

I remained silent as I waited for paperwork to be completed and then was secured onto a gurney for the paramedics to wheel me out to their ambulance. Once safely inside one of the medics was going over my paperwork, I began to break down. "Why me, Lord? Why me?" Though the medic was there with me, I felt so helpless and alone. My only constant sense of comfort for the last months of my anguish had waltzed out of the hospital nearly an hour before with the devil he called his father. I missed my son already. I was tired and overwhelmed by everything that was happening. A greater pain could never be known to mankind.

"Ma'am, you've got to calm down," the medic told me as his partner whipped the ambulance through the busy city streets. "I need you to stop crying, okay? Everything is going to be okay."

I couldn't believe all this was happening. I knew that the medic meant well by telling me that things would be okay, but the truth was that he didn't know what all I'd endured and since no one knew what was wrong with me he also had no clue as to how my story would end. The drive to K&T Hospital took forty-five minutes. Huge doors were opened up for us as we pulled in the driveway.

"We're here," the medic advised me as his partner ran to the back of the ambulance to open its doors.

The duo lowered my gurney and wheeled me through the large open doors of the hospital. They found a place to put me, had me sign a form, and gave me warm smiles filled with encouragement.

"Okay, ma'am," the one who'd been in back with me stated. "Someone will be with you shortly. I pray for the best for you."

"Thank you," I told him.

Minutes after they'd left me a nurse headed in my direction. For a moment I was sure she was going to stop in front of me, but when she didn't I felt discouraged. "Miss?" I called out to her.

The nurse turned around and approached me. "Yes, Ma'am?"

"I need help. No one has been able to figure out what is wrong with me. I'm not from here so I don't know anything about this hospital, its doctor's or anything…do you think they will be able to help me here?"

I knew that my question sounded naïve and pitiful but the nurse gave me a reassuring smile. "Yes, my dear! K&T has some of the best doctors in the south." She winked at me, reached for my hand, and gave it a squeeze. "It'll be fine."

With just her few kind words I felt a lot more comfortable. In fact, everyone I had encountered at K&T were really nice. At some point an admissions representative found me and had me sign my medical consent forms. After that a young nurse placed me in a wheelchair and wheeled me up to my room. The room was a huge room with a big TV and a phone. I liked it already. I was very tired from the ride into Texas the day before and the commute from the military hospital to this one. I was ready to lie down and rest in the peace and stillness of the sterile room. Before I could shut my eyes there was a knock on my room door. The young nurse, Carrie, was back with a wheelchair.

"You ready, sweetie?" Nurse Carrie asked.

I gave her a blank expression. Did she not realize that she'd just delivered me to my room not even fifteen minutes ago? "Huh!? Ready for what?"

"We have to take you down to get a CT Scan and some X-rays."

I sighed. "Sure...unless I have a choice."

She smiled at me. “No, ma’am. The only choice you have is to come with me. You want to know what’s going on right?”

She had a point there. I went through the motions and endured the full battery of imaging that was done in a pursuit of figuring out the mystery behind my ailments. It was late afternoon when they finally rolled me back in my room. I was starving by then so I asked the nurse if they were going to feed me.

“Hmmm, not right now,” Nurse Carrie answered as she helped me get back into bed. “Someone will be over shortly to get some labs from you and run a few more tests.”

I was astonished. “How many more test can there be?” I was beyond exhausted and was beginning to feel like a human lab experiment.

“We’ve got to be thorough,” she replied before exiting the room.

Later, around 10 PM I was back in my room from completing what felt like every blood test created and various culture strips. Now that I had starved for so long, I was no longer hungry. It was finally time for me to lay down and get some rest. There was nothing more to be done or said for the day and I welcomed the opportunity to close my eyes. Unfortunately, the opportunity did not occur. Each hour Nurse Carrie wandered into my room to draw a fresh round of labs.

"Do I really have enough blood for you to do every single hour?" I complained during the 12 AM round. "This is crazy."

She worked as quickly as she could, drawing blood from my arm almost effortlessly. "I'm sorry. But again, we've got to be thorough."

I appreciated their attention to detail and making sure that no stone went unturned in an effort to help me, but I was exhausted beyond belief. Since I wasn't able to go to sleep, I decided to call J. I hadn't heard from him all night and he certainly hadn't made his way up with my clothes as he'd promised.

"What?" he said upon answering the phone.

I ignored his attitude. "Are you coming up here or not?"

"No," he said with little or no remorse. "I won't be back til tomorrow. I've been stuck in ridiculous track all day between coming back home, taking Trey to my mom, and then coming back home."

I was disappointed but I also understood his frustration. Besides, I would much rather him go home and regroup instead of coming up to the hospital pissed because of how his day had gone and taking it out on me. "Well, take down this number. It's my room phone number."

"Okay."

"And my room number is 2110 when you get up here," I said in a weary tone.

"Okay. I got it."

I hesitated, noticing that he never once asked me how I was feeling or if I'd learned anything new in his absence. "Okay, well…sleep well."

"Yeah," he said before disconnecting the call.

I hung up the receiver and forced myself to block out my physical and emotional discomfort.

After a while I became immune to Nurse Carrie's comings and goings. I slept better than I had in days. By the time I woke up I was confused about where I was. After a few moments all of the memories from the day before returned to me. I sighed and tried to adjust my pillows. My eyes fell upon the chair to the right of me and I recognized my overnight bag immediately. I was stunned. Apparently J had been there, but looking around the room I saw no other traces of him. I waited, holding my breath for a few moments, to see if he would emerge from the bathroom in my room or saunter in through my room door. After a while I realized that he was simply not there.

Knock, knock. I was becoming accustomed to the continuous raps upon my room door.

"Come in," I called out.

In walked a lab tech. "Hi, I'm Becca. I'm here to get your hourly blood work."

I wondered where Nurse Carrie was but I didn't say a word.

"Just to let you know, you have a couple of appointments scheduled for today so you want to be sure to rest in between whenever possible," Becca advised.

I nodded my understanding. "No problem so long as you all are going to get me well."

She smiled at me. "That's the plan."

An hour later there was another knock on the door and twenty-five people dressed in white coats entered my room and surrounded my bed. I sat up straight, afraid of what was about to happen next. I instantly thought that perhaps whatever was wrong with me was so bad that they needed a large team to treat it. One of the doctors walked over to me and shook my hand. "Good morning, Ms. January. I'm Dr. Dennis and these guys are my med students. Do we have your consent for them to stand in during our visit this morning?"

I didn't know what to say. "Umm…okay. I guess so."

"K&T Hospital is a teaching hospital and these particular students are on clinical. They have to have so many hours of clinical instruction."

"Oh, I see."

Done with his explanation, Dr. Dennis then rattled off my stats, including name, age, last vitals recorded and the reason for my stay was currently inconclusive. Moments later the entire tribe filed right back out of my room and went off to visit another patient. Soon after another nurse, Crystal, whom I learned was Nurse Carrie's shift change replacement, came to transport me to my first appointment. All of the specialists that I visited that day were located in the lower part of the hospital where various physicians' suites were located. After being poked and probed, questioned and stared at, all of my appointments were over and I was returned to my room where Nurse Crystal advised me that I was being transferred to another floor. The way that I was being moved around from here to there was beginning to upset me. But, I was silent as she helped me into a wheelchair and took me up exactly one floor.

We arrived to an open floor. There was no phone, no TV, not even a window or doors to separate one patient's space from another.

"What type of room is this?" I asked, surprised that they would just dump me there like that.

Nurse Crystal wheeled me over to a bed saying nothing.

"There isn't anywhere for me put my stuff?" I asked referring to the bag of clothes that J had left for me.

"They'll store it for you in a closet downstairs," Nurse Crystal replied. "No worries, everything is going to be just fine. You're not even allowed to wear your own clothes, so you'll just keep on the gown that you're in."

I was instantly turned off by the environment. It was ice cold up there and I was freezing. "Why is it so cold in here?" I complained she flipped through my chart.

"Melissa…Baby girl, it's only temporary."

I didn't care how temporary she felt it was, I was unhappy. I wanted to scream how I couldn't understand why they were taking me away from my nice, cozy room with a TV and a phone in order to put me into this freezer. I felt like my days were numbered. Suddenly fear consumed me. *Is this where they put people who are about to die*, I wondered. I looked around at all of the bleak faces of the other patients who laid on their beds moaning in agony, staring at the pale yellow walls, or crying with their eyes shut. *Oh, God! My days must really be numbered.* I wondered how much longer I had and if I would be able to get in touch with J in time for him to bring my son so that I could at least say goodbye to him. I began to get teary eyed thinking of the possibility of not being able to hug and kiss my boy one more time. I never thought that I would die alone. No one even knew where I was. All my friends and family members were in other places in the world. I had no one to hold my hand, no on to comfort me, and no one to share my final wishes with. I wondered if the doctors had even bothered to contact J and tell him that I was dying since they certainly hadn't bothered to formally share the information with me.

As I remained in my bed on the open floor I was afraid that I would die any minute. I must have fallen asleep during my tearful and unyielding praying. When I woke up and it felt even colder. I pushed the button on the side of my bed to signal the nurse. Within moments a red-haired woman appeared.

"Yes, Ma'am?" she asked politely.

"I need another blanket," I told her while trembling. "It is so cold in here."

She nodded and trotted off to retrieve the blanket. Moments later she returned with one and covered me up. Still, my body felt like it was freezing.

"Why y'all have it so cold in here?" I screamed as my teeth chattered. "Or is it me? Am I dying? Please tell me," I begged, no longer wanting to be kept in the dark about the truth. "Somebody tell me something before I freak out."

The nurse patted my hand and spoke in a hushed tone. "Calm down. There are other patients on this floor and they are asleep. This is only temporary."

There was that word again. Was it only temporary because they expected me to die soon? “But why is it so cold?” I asked again.

“Because it’s an open floor.”

Before I could say another word, Dr. Dennis appeared by the nurse’s side. “How are you feeling, Melissa?”

“Cold, tired, and uncomfortable,” I told him. “My body…it’s just tired and achy.”

“We’re unable to give you any kind of meds right now because we’re waiting on some lab results to come back. But, I can tell you that based on the imaging results it’s probably best if we remove your gallbladder.”

“What? My gallbladder?” I’d heard of the organ but I wasn’t really sure what its function was.”

“Yes, Ma’am. The jaundice, uh…the yellowing of your eyes, your pain after consuming food, and the nausea are all signs of an inflamed gallbladder. Even the chills that you’re experiencing are a common symptom. We’re going to have to remove it in order to get you some relief.”

“Surgery,” I stated.

He nodded. “Yes, Ma’am. Someone will be by to go over some paperwork with you and the procedure okay?” He patted my arm. “Try to relax and get some rest.”

I was relieved to know that the doctor had an answer for me but I wasn’t thrilled about the idea of surgery. At least I’m not dying, I thought. When the nurse came back around with the paperwork, I wasted no time in signing my consent for the removal of my gallbladder. I didn’t even bother to look over the papers that she put before me. I just knew that I wanted this process over and done with.

The next morning, I woke up around 4 AM, shaking and completely freezing. Looking down at my arms I found myself connected to all kinds of tubes. As I tried to piece together what had happened a nurse walked in.

“Oh,” she said sounding startled. “You’re awake. Are you okay?”

“What is all of this stuff?” I asked her, referring to the tubes dangling around me.

"Precautions," she stated. "Standard necessities but it's only temporary. After your surgery everything is going to get removed."

I closed my eyes upon hearing the word temporary. I assumed that all of the medical staff had been trained to recite that line because I swore that it was the answer to nearly all of my questions. I must have gone back to sleep because when I woke up again I was laying on the table in the operating room. Dr. Dennis and a sea of nurses dressed in green scrubs were bustling around preparing for the procedure.

"Are you ready?" Dr. Dennis asked me.

I swallowed hard. "Yes."

"I know your nurse went over this, but we're just going to cover it once more before we get started, okay?"

I nodded. The doctor proceeded to explain to me everything that they were going to do. I tried to focus on him but my body began to feel clammy. As he spoke he looked into my eyes and realized that something wasn't right. He looked over at the monitor beside me and checked my blood pressure.

"Ready doctor?" a nurse asked with the anesthesiologist standing beside her.

"Let's get her temperature one more time," Dr. Dennis stated.

The nurse was surprised but she followed orders. She used a handheld device which she swiped across my face until a beep occurred. "Oh wow," she stated. "107."

"Melissa," the doctor called to me. "We're going to have to get your fever down before we can operate. We'll give it some time and then reschedule your surgery, okay?"

I was so distraught that I couldn't respond. It was just one set back after another. It was bad enough that I was undergoing a surgical procedure without a support system nearby, but now my agony was being delayed because my body wouldn't cooperate. They returned me to my bed on the open floor and continuously supplied me with popsicles while sponging me down with cold water. An hour later my fever was down to 100 degrees so the doctor agreed to proceed with the surgery.

***

The light bothered my eyes as I tried to open them. My mouth felt dry. Turning over to my left I saw my husband who looked none too pleased to see me peering back at him. My spirit couldn't take the scowl on his face so I turned my head to the right and saw my sister Charlene. Was I dreaming? Somewhere from another corner of the room I heard my other sister, Denise, talking to someone else. I wasn't sure what was going on or why my sisters were there from Georgia. I looked back to J and that disappointed look etched across his face. I didn't know what his issue was and I didn't care too much at the same time. I wanted to say something to them all but the moment I tried I realized that I couldn't.

"Sweetie, can you hear me?" Charlene asked me as she moved closer to my bed and took a seat on the edge.

I nodded my head yes. Words just would not escape my mouth.

She reached for my limp hand. "Press my hand as hard as you can for ten seconds."

I didn't understand the test, but I complied.

As I squeezed, she counted "1, 2, 3, 4, 5, 6, 7, 8,9,10."

I gave it all I could even though I couldn't feel the pressure I was working hard to apply.

"Yes!" Charlene screamed. She jumped up and turned her back to me. "She did it, Doctor! She did it! Now can we please take the tube out.?"

I had no clue what she was talking about but as I looked around all I saw were monitors, tubes, and cables everywhere. I could not believe it. I was hooked up to far more stuff than I'd questioned the nurse about before my surgery. *Now can we take the tube out*, I thought. *What tube? Which tube?* My eyes grew wide in wonderment. I was oblivious to what was going on but the longer the scene played out the more I knew that it wasn't a dream.

The doctor approached my bedside with his plastic gloved hands and methodically removed a large tube that had been lodged down my throat. No wonder I couldn't speak. In my confused state I hadn't even realized that something was hanging from inside of my mouth. Once he removed the tube I began to vomit vehemently and uncontrollably. Spurts of puke splattered onto the doctor's white coat and all over the sheets of my bed.

"It's okay, it's okay," Dr. Dennis assured me. "That's normal," he said looking around at the concerned faces of my sisters. "Don't worry. The nurses will take care of it and get her cleaned up."

Just as he said, a tech came into the room and assisted the staff nurse in cleaning me up and changing my sheets. Once they were done I had very little time to spend with my sisters before the nurse advised that my visitors had to leave.

Denise came over and hugged me long and hard. "We have to get back to Atlanta, sweetie."

I was shocked. I'd seen them all of thirty minutes and now they were heading back home. It didn't' make sense to me. I wondered why they'd even come there in the first place.

"The doctors said everything is going to be fine," Denise advised. She hugged me again. "It's going to be okay. Okay?"

I was still unable to talk so I just nodded.

Charlene came to me next and hugged me as well. "We're going to see you soon, okay? Get well soon. I love you."

My sisters took a final look at me and made their way to the door. I looked over at my husband. The sour expression on his face remained and he offered me no explanation as to what was going on.

"I have to take them to the airport now," he stated. "I'll be back later."

I wondered if his look of disdain had anything to do with the reason why my sisters had made the trip to Texas yet were leaving so abruptly.

***

The next day I was awakened by a few doctors greeting me and telling me that I looked so great. I couldn't understand why they keep staring at me and smiling at the same time. Once the doctors left out I paged for a nurse.

"Good morning," Nurse Carrie greeted me.

I was glad to see a familiar staff member. I opened my mouth to speak but the words would not come out.

"Are you okay?" Nurse Carrie asked.

I shook my head. I was frustrated because I could not communicate. I was able to think intelligent thoughts but I was unable to relay them.

"Relax, relax," Nurse Carrie suggested. "It's going to take a minute for everything to get back to normal, but just relax. This is only temporary."

I closed my eyes and fought back the tears. I loathed that empty line they continued to feed me.

"How about a nice bath?" Nurse Carrie stated.

Unable to ask for anything else or do anything else I simply nodded.

She gave me a bath in bed and I noticed that she kept looking at me and patting my cheek. I felt more helpless and lost than I ever had. That familiar feeling of freezing returned after my bath. Day after day I laid in that freezing room with no visitors, no phone, no TV, and no clue as to what was really going on. It bothered me that the doctors would only marvel over how good I looked each day. No one seemed concerned with explaining to me why it was that I couldn't speak.

Three days later I was being transferred to a regular floor with a phone. Determined to force my speech to return, the first thing I did once settled into my private room was to call my son. He was still with my mother-in-law in Houston. Once she answered her cell phone only one word could escape my tongue.

"Trey," I said weakly.

"Hold on, hold on," Ms. Christine said hurriedly.

I heard shuffling and then moments later the greatest sound on earth filled my ears. "Mommy! I love you Ma-Ma! Miss you Ma-Ma."

I gripped the receiver tightly and pressed my eye lids shut even tighter. I knew that I had to work through the discomfort I felt to relay the most important message I ever had drifting through my head and heart. "Mommy loves you too and I can't wait to see you."

I listened to him chatter for a little while longer as I was unable to say much but soon Ms. Christine retuned to the line.

"How are you doing over there, Melissa?"

"Better," I managed to say.

She spoke for a while, telling me how Trey was doing just fine and was eager to see me again. Our call ended soon after and I wanted to call my sisters in Atlanta but I couldn't remember their phone numbers. How could I remember one number that I hadn't known very long but not the numbers that I'd known forever? *What's happening*, I wondered. *What's wrong with my memory?*

That night J came for a visit. He entered the room and immediately turned the television on to watch his favorite TV show. "You need anything?" he asked before taking a seat.

I shook my head deciding not to strain my voice.

He sat and watched his show in peace and I lay in bed consumed with my own thoughts. It was really as if he wasn't there. He stayed for an hour and then left without saying much of anything.

Soon after Nurse Carrie entered the room. "Okay, sweetie! Let's take a bath."

I was glad to see her. Her spirit was so uplifting and the thought of doing something other than wallowing in my own self-pity and confusion sparked my excitement. I threw the covers back and looked down at my two huge elephant-looking legs. I immediately started crying. "What is this?" I struggled to whisper through my tears. "My legs. My legs are the size of an elephant's!" I looked up at Nurse Carrie for an explanation.

"Sweetie, you've been through a lot," she told me. "But you will be just fine."

I began to inspect my body, taking notice of things that I haven't been aware of before. I screamed when I saw that my arms were huge too. I touched my face. "My face," I said. "My face! My Face!"

"Relax, sweetie. Relax!" Nurse Carrie insisted. "It's fine."

"Nooooooooo!!!" I screamed. My heart was breaking as I lost control. I tried to get of bed but found it to be a struggle. "Oh my God! I'm paralyzed. I'm paralyzed." I was able to move my arms but not my legs.

Nurse Carrie was right by my side. She put my arm around her shoulders and helped me up off of the bed. "See," she said, walking me slowly over to an awaiting wheel chair. "You're not paralyzed, sweetie. You've just been through a lot."

I took a seat in the wheelchair and looked up at her in a panic. "What? What is it? What have I been through?"

She took a deep breath and gave me an empathic look. "Someone will let you know soon." She wheeled me on to the bathroom. As we passed by the sink I saw myself in the mirror for the first time. "Oh God!" I broke down. I was huge.

I demanded that she weigh me, so Nurse Carrie took me to a scale on the unit where I was able to sit and weighed. When the number read 305 I couldn't trust my eyes. I became a mental wreck. Nurse Carrie took me back to my room, finished my bath and helped me back into bed where she reconnected all of the machines.

"Get some rest, honey," she told me. "I'll see you tomorrow."

She left me there alone with all of my thoughts and fears. *Am I am going to die*, I wondered. I still had no clue what it was that was wrong with me now. They'd removed my gallbladder so that was no longer an issue. I couldn't phantom what the issue could be. I closed my eyes and did the only thing that I knew to do--I prayed.

***

Knock, knock. "Good morning! How are you, sweetheart?" Nurse Carrie asked in her usual upbeat tone as she entered the room.

"Terrible," I mumbled. "I need someone to tell me what's happening."

"Dr. Xu will be here later to explain everything to you, okay?"

Who the heck is that, I thought. I was certain that my issue was no longer with my gallbladder since it wasn't Dr. Dennis who was coming by to speak with me. I couldn't wait for Dr. Xu to knock on my door so that I could get some answers.

I didn't have to wait long. Shortly after Nurse Carrie checked my vitals, the door opened and in walked a short, Asian man. He took one look at me and smiled so wide that his eyes slanted to a nearly closed position. "Oh wow! Melissa, you look great."

I was sick of hearing that. "No I don't look great, Doctor. I look like a gorilla right now. I am huge and my body is all kinds of colors. I'm fat. And I hurt, Dr. Xu. All I want to do is cry." Even as I said the words, the water works began to spark.

Dr. Xu sat down the chart in his hands and took hold of both of my hands. "Let's just pray for a minute."

I was so astounded by his liberalness. He was a doctor, not a preacher and he wanted to sit down and pray with me. I knew that it was completely unorthodox for medical professionals to engage in any religious acts with patients. The moment reminded me of the day I'd had my C-section to commence Trey's birth. I felt better immediately knowing that I had a doctor that was concerned about my mental, emotional, and spiritual well-being as well as my physical health. Tears of joy rolled down my face as the doctor led us in a prayer so touching that I just knew our savior was present in that room.

"I want you to know that I truly care about you Melissa and want you to feel better," he told me. "You are an amazing person with a beautiful spirit."

I felt touched by his kindness.

"Please, I want you to meet my wife," he stated, rising from his seated position on my bed and hurrying to the door where he motioned for someone.

Seconds later, in walked a short, plump woman with her hair pulled back into a ponytail that flowed down her back.

"This is my wife Shoshanna," Dr. Xu explained. "We've been married for fifteen years." He smiled proudly as he made the announcement. I admired the sincerity of his love for his wife. I wondered if J had ever smiled so proudly and if his eyes had ever shined brightly when speaking for me.

Shoshanna hugged me as if she'd known me a full lifetime. Her embrace felt genuine and it touched my soul. I wondered who exactly were these people and why were they so loving and caring. Shoshanna excused herself after telling me how nice it was to meet me and Dr. Xu got back to business.

"Melissa, you have been through a lot," he said.

"So I keep being told," I retorted. "But I don't understand what has happened."

"We're just so glad to see that you are doing so well. When Dr. Dennis removed your gallbladder the procedure was done through your belly button. Once the gallbladder was out, there was a lot of fluid inside of your body that was harmful. The surgical team wasn't able to control what was going on. So much seemed to happen at once from having fluid in your lungs to internal bleeding right down to an inflamed liver."

I gasped. My entire body seemed to have gone haywire and I hadn't even known it.

"It appears that you suffer from Autoimmune Hepatitis. Are you familiar with that term at all?" he asked me.

I nodded slightly. "I was told that I had it as a child…I was maybe sixteen. I thought it was done…that it had cured itself—"

"It's one of those things that will most likely come and go for a lifetime, Melissa. And it's pretty much driven by the inflammation of your liver. Your immune system was attacking it. These things are greatly stressed related."

I was devastated. Was he saying that I would be sick off and on forever?

"So after that happened we didn't know where to start and what to attend to first so we were forced to put you into a medically induced medical coma which usually lasts about twenty-four hours," he said.

"Usually?" I asked, raising an eyebrow.

"Yes, but that was not the case with you. We waited twenty-four hours but there was no response from your body. You were here mentally but not physically. We could see minimal brain activity on the monitor."

My eyes grew wide as he continued to explain the situation to me.

"There was no response from you until three months later."

"What!" I screamed, staring at him in disbelief. "Three…three months. I looked around the room to see if anything appeared different to me. "Three months? I've been here for three months?"

"The doctors who operated on you didn't see there being a chance of you living. You were placed on my caseload and me and my wife visited you every day. We prayed for your return. We prayed over you…we prayed with your family. We knew that God had a greater plan for you and death was not it."

I was in total shock. I couldn't believe it. It all made sense now--why my sisters were there and why everyone kept telling me how good I looked considering I'd been in a coma for three months.

"Your weight gain can be attributed to the side effects of the medications we've administered to you daily through this tube." He pointed to the IV in my right arm. "The prednisone and cortisone. You are experiencing difficulty in walking because your whole body was shut down for three months. It will take time for you to regain that strength and mobility. Soon you will be able to work with a physical therapist who is going to get you back on your feet."

"Wow," I said as I took it all in. "Thank you, Dr. Xu. And please, please thank your wife for me too. Thank you both for being there for me." I realized that my family or the hospital could have pulled the plug on me months ago since Dr. Dennis and his staff hadn't felt I would survive the coma. "Thank you for explaining it all to me."

Now that I knew what had happened and where I was at the time, I felt that I could start working on rebuilding my life. My memory was returning and I was able to remember Charlene's phone number. I called her the moment Dr. Xu left my room.

"Did you know?" I asked her after we got past all of the pleasantries.

"Yes," she admitted. "But your doctor said that it was best for us not to tell you anything so that you wouldn't have a break down."

I couldn't help but to think how bad of an idea that was. The not knowing what was wrong was what happened to be torturing me the most. "Well, now that I know I can work on getting back on my feet."

"Take it slow, sis," Charlene advised.

"I will," I promised.

Once our call ended, I called J but of course he didn't answer. I knew now more than ever that everything happened for a reason. I had a new chance at life and I wasn't about to let J and his foolery alter my mood.

Three days later Dr. Xu was sending me home. He stood in my room with my discharge papers in hand and a smile on his face.

On my face rested a frown. "No," I told him, remembering what my home life was like. "I don't think I'll be able to function at my home."

Dr. Xu waved off my concern. "You have your husband there and I'm sure he will help you with everything."

If he only knew, I thought.

We went over my discharge instructions and Dr. Xu advised me that within the next two hours the nurse would come by to officially let me go. I called J to let him know what was going on.

"They're discharging me today," I told him.

"Why?" he asked in shock.

"I don't know. Dr. Xu just told me. I think it's crazy too."

"That's just great," he seethed through the phone.

I knew that J wasn't too happy about me coming back home and that was fine with me. I was just ready to see my little man.

"You can't even take care of yourself. I damn sure don't have time to be bothered with you."

I took a deep breath and forced myself not to allow him to affect me. “Can you please come pick me up? They’re discharging me at nine.”

He just hung up without responding. I wondered what it was that he had to be so angry about when I was the one in the messed up condition. He had a break from me for almost four months.

Soon after, the nurse arrived to disconnect me from the catheter and the tubes that were still connected to my body. It felt good to be free of all the extra stuff dangling from my body. The nurse helped me to pack my things so that I would be ready to go when my ride arrived. I still had difficulty walking. Dr. Xu told me to follow up with him in the next three weeks. He also let me know that a physical therapist was scheduled to come to my house three to five times a week. Dr. Xu seemed really convinced in my ability to thrive outside of the hospital already. Even though I really liked him, I thought it was strange that he was discharging me three days after awakening from a coma. I wasn’t even mobile yet and I couldn’t do anything on my own.

At 9 AM the nurse returned with a wheelchair to transport me out of the room. With my little bag in my lap I sat in the hallway of the floor of the recovery ward waiting. Ten minutes into my wait the nurse came to me with concern.

"What time is your husband coming?"

I could not even give her an answer. I was ashamed so I just told her that he was going to be there soon. I sat there long enough to watch the next shift of nurses come in. I knew that it had to be past 3 PM. The nurses all asked me how I was doing and if I was going home as they passed my pitiful body waiting patiently in the hallway. My one, rehearsed answer was always, "Yes, Ma'am. My husband should be here soon."

I sat in the hallway nearly all day as visitors passed by me to check in on their loved ones or friends. Having grown bored with waiting, I asked one of the nurses to push me down the hall so that I could watch some TV. The sun was going down and it started to get dark outside. I knew it was late in the evening by now. I asked a nurse if I could call my husband to see if he was on his way or if he was still coming. J didn't answer the phone so I just hung up and tried again. After trying three more times I gave up, leaving him a voice message asking him to please let me know what time he was coming or if he was coming at all.

He never bothered to call the hospital back to let me know anything. The nightshift nurses had taken the floor and I was still there. One of the nurses took a look at me and inquired as to what was going on.

"What are you still doing here, Melissa?" she asked. "I thought you were discharged this morning."

I burst out in tears. I knew that it was almost midnight.

"Whoa, whoa, whoa. What's wrong, dear?"

I looked her in the eyes and told the pitiful truth. "I called my husband at 7 AM this morning and told him that I was going to be discharged at 9 AM and he is still not here."

She hugged me. "Aww sweetheart. Have you called him since then?"

"Yes, ma'am. Five times and he would not answer so I was only able to leave him a message. I've been sitting here in this chair all day and I'm in so much pain."

"Well we can at least do something about that," the nurse said. She gave me some meds so I could calm down and told me that stressing would only make matters worse. She told me to relax and that she'd be back soon.

Before I knew it the meds kicked in. I felt myself calming down and feeling less stressed. It was a quiet night for the nurse so she came back and sat with me. By 1 AM, I realized that I'd been sitting in that wheelchair for nearly sixteen hours without anything to drink or to eat. My body was in pain and I was more pissed off than ever at J's nerve.

At 1:45 AM, J and two security guards came walking down the hallway.

"There he goes!" I said, rather stunned to see him at all.

The nurse watched as he approached us. "That's good. Maybe he just had to work late," the nurse said.

I couldn't believe my eyes. After all of the hours that he'd made me wait, J had finally waltzed into the hospital at a time when visiting hours were over. "How did you get in the hospital this late?" I asked him. But before he could respond, I held up my hand. "Let me stop. I'm not even going to start. Just get me out of here."

J wheeled me out of the unit and then out of the hospital. He put me in the car never once asking me how I was doing. It was an hour ride home with no words spoken between the two of us. Once home, he parked the truck in the garage, got out, and then simply walked into the house. For a moment I thought he was going inside to get something or just to open some doors to make the transition easier. But, after a while I realized that he was just being and inconsiderate ass. He knew that I could not move or get out of the truck by myself. I waited for about ten minutes until he finally came back out.

"Are you coming in?" he asked.

I was dumbfounded. “I can’t! You have to help me.”

“See, I knew this shit wasn’t going to work out!” he ranted. “You can’t do shit on your own. Why the hell they send you home and you can’t do shit?” While he carried me out of the truck he continued complaining about how ugly and fat I was and how disgusting I smelled.

I endured his verbal abuse until he literally threw me into the armchair in the living room.

“Where I supposed to sleep?” I asked him. “Certainly not here.”

“Not in my bed,” he replied. “Stay in the damn chair.” He exited the room and left me alone.

I promised myself I wasn’t going to get upset anymore. There were no lights on in the living room and the TV was off. I just sat in the chair thinking about everything that had happened to me since getting with this man. All of a sudden I felt like I had to pee. It came with so much pressure that I felt my body straining to hold it to end. I remembered how I hadn’t moved in over sixteen hours before J decided to come get me. During that time, I hadn't used the restroom and now my bladder was overly full. I couldn't get out of the chair on my own,

"J!" I screamed his name so that he could come help. "J, come get me out of this chair! I have to pee!"

He didn't stir at all. In my frustration I screamed for him again. "J, please!" I was unable to hold it. Feeling humiliated and childish, I peed in my clothes on the chair. Tears dripped from my eyes as the warm urine soaked my bottom and thighs. I clenched tightly in an effort to cut off the stream. I did not want to just sit there and let it all out on myself so I mustered up all of my strength and stood from the chair only to fall straight onto the floor. Without anything or anyone to help me balance myself I landed with a thud.

I punched the floor in anger. I couldn't get myself back up off of the floor. Desperate, I rolled myself over and over until I was close to the hallway bathroom and from there I crawled into the bathroom. Pulling myself up against the sink, I was able to push myself onto the toilet. But, by the time I'd gone through all of that I'd already peed all over myself. Sitting there helplessly drenched from my piss, I called for my husband yet again.

"J! I need your help! Please!" I begged loudly. "Please help me into the tub."

After screaming back and forth for about ten minutes, he finally got up and ran my bath water. Reluctantly, he lifted me off of the toilet seat and just threw me into the hot water. Immediately my skin began to wrinkle from the heat of the water. I had wounds all over my body from all of the tubes that I had been attached from the numerous surgeries I'd had. My whole body started to burn immediately at those wound sites as a result of the scolding hot water. After a few minutes I could not take it any longer.

"Get me out! Get me out!" I screamed as if I was dying.

J walked in and pulled me out of the tub and placed me on the toilet seat. He scowled at me. "Happy?"

"Can I get a towel, please." it pained me that I had to ask him for help."

He stormed off yet returned with a towel and gave me a look of disgust. "Oh wow! You look like a whale. What the hell did they feed you in the hospital?"

I blocked out his ranting wile I struggled to dry off as he helped me to the bedroom and into clean clothes. Laying my head against my pillows, I closed my eyes and it didn't take long for me to drift off. My prayer that night was very short. "Lord, please keep me for tonight and let me awake in the morning! AMEN!

~ Chapter 6~

Trying to Function

"I can't change the direction of the wind, but I can adjust my sails to always reach my destination."

-Jimmy Dean

J was gone when I woke up around 7 AM. He must have left early to go to work. There was no food in the house, no water or juice to drink, and no one for me to call to help me. I figured that he would at least come home around lunch time to check on me. Looking around I noticed that in the four months that my husband had to unpack all of our stuff, absolutely nothing had been done. I wondered what it was that he did every day after work. I was done with him. He'd gotten me to a point where I just couldn't tolerate his behavior any longer. Had I been in better shape I would have just gotten up then and there to leave, but I wasn't so I couldn't.

The only thing that seemed to be unwrapped and put in its place was the TV. Rummaged through boxes and fully closed boxes were everywhere. All of my stuff was still packed away and stored in my son's room. Judging by the way nothing was done and the lack of food in the kitchen, I deducted that the house appeared completely unlived in for surely he couldn't have been surviving this way.

He didn't come home until later on that night around 9:45 PM when I heard the door. He came in fully dressed in jeans, a T-shirt, and some tennis shoes. It was obvious that he wasn't returning from work. He said nothing to me as if I wasn't even there.

Trying to be cordial, I decided to break the ice. "Hey, how are you?"

"What you want?" he asked, stepping out of his sneakers.

I took a deep breath and just got right down to it. "I would like to know how I am supposed to survive in this house. There is no food and I've have been sucking ice cubes all day just to stay hydrated. It's not like I am able to eat huge loads of food, but I need something in my stomach."

"I don't have any money right now to grocery shop," he replied nonchalantly. "I been sending all my money to my mom to take care of Trey while you been laying up in the hospital racking up medical expenses."

"Really?" I was stunned because when I last spoke to his mom she told me that he was not helping her at all with food or clothes for Trey. Clearly someone wasn't being truthful. "Can you please get my medicine for me?" I asked, changing the subject to ward off his attitude. "I was supposed to start taking it last night."

"Yes." He huffed deeply but still trudged off to the kitchen to get my medication. He brought it back to the room and tossed it towards me in the chair.

"Thank you," I responded meekly.

He reached into his pockets and produced a couple of bills. "And here is some money for some water and some crackers," he said, tossing the dollars my way.

I watched as he changed clothes wondering just how he expected me to get to the store to get the items he'd given me money for. Once he was changed he headed for the door. "I'll be back," he said over his shoulder without further explanation.

He returned after two hours. I did not say a word. I just took my meds and tried to forget that he was even in the house. I didn't want to watch television or read a book. I just wanted to sleep and ignore J. Although there was no food in the house it didn't matter because my appetite was all the way jacked up off of the medicine I was taking. The entire scenario made me just want to sleep and never wake up again. *God, I did not sign up to live like this*, I prayed in my head. *Can you just please come and get me? I can't take this any longer.* My whole body was in pain. I knew that I couldn't do anything by myself or for myself. To make matters worse, my son was not with me and my family was miles and miles away. I needed someone to help me. I needed somebody to relieve me from all of the pain that was plaguing me. I didn't want to live like this anymore.

I must have fallen asleep for a couple of minutes because when I woke up he was gone again. I tried to get up but I couldn't. I was too weak. My body was burning and the pain from sitting in the chair all day was excruciating. I couldn't do it any longer. I felt like I was getting worse by the minute. I pushed myself all the way to the front of the chair and got up slowly. I exhaled deeply before trying to make any other movements. Step by step, I held my hands out with nothing but air to grasp. Suddenly, I lost my balance and fell onto the floor made of cold, stone tiles. I knew that I couldn't lay there for too long so I pushed myself back up to the chair and this time I pivoted myself towards the sofa where I could lay down and stretch out. Exhausted, I struggled to get my cup of melted ice off of the coffee table and pulled my pain killers out of my pocket. With my heart racing, I swallowed down a pill and settled in for an uncomfortable sleep.

The next day when I awoke he was actually home. I was surprised. "When will you be able to pick up Trey?" I asked as he settled down to watch T.V. "I really miss him. I haven't seen him in almost a half a year. I know he's probably all big now." It saddened me that he hadn't even shown me pictures of our son to ease my heartache.

"You can't take care of him so I'm not going to go get him," he responded.

Although his statement was true, it still hurt. "But how about yourself? You don't miss him?"

"I speak to him," he said. "I've been to visit."

That gave me an idea. "Well, could you just pick him up for one weekend for me?"

"Considering that it's about a seven-hour drive back and forth…Nope!" he answered heartlessly.

I studied his face as he stared straight ahead at the television. There I was again getting mad over the same things—no food in this house, boxes everywhere, no phone, and an uncaring husband. How much more devastating could life get? Feeling the anger rising in me, I realized that once again I need to get to the restroom. Each time I'd tried to take myself it was catastrophic. I tried my best to hold it until J was around to assist, although he was never pleased to do so.

"Can you help me to the bathroom?" I asked softly.

"Why?" he whined.

"Because I have to pee!"

He took too long to get up so I ended up peeing on myself again. I said nothing as the hot stream drenched my clothing. Finally, he rose to assist me but the moment he looked at me his face filled with anger and madness. His expression was devastating to me and made me feel worse than I already did.

"It's not my fault," I began to defend myself. "Why did it take you so long? I can't really control my pee anymore. It's hard to hold it, especially for as long as I have been. It's like it just runs out."

"It's not easy for me either," he snapped. "Best believe it. Dealing with you is like having another child. What you come home for Melissa if you can't even function?"

"I didn't want to come home," I told him truthfully. There were several reasons why I would have preferred to stay in the hospital. "They just kicked me out. I told them I wasn't ready." I tried to hold back my tears but was unsuccessful. "Can you run me some bath water please?" I asked with my head held down.

Again he asked, "Why the hell would you leave the hospital knowing you can't do anything by yourself? You can't take care of yourself!"

"It was not my decision for the hospital to discharge me," I countered. Was he ever going to understand that? I shook my head in disbelief. "If I could have stayed best believe I would have…Who wants to be home, well in *this* home because this here doesn't even feel like *a* home. I feel like I'm trapped in some cage or something!"

He grabbed me very harshly by the shoulders, pulling me out of the chair. My legs, arms, and nearly every part of my body were hurting so every shake he inflicted upon me via his vice grip was painful. I could feel the hatred he had for me as he dragged me to the bathroom. He held me roughly as the water poured and he undressed me, and then dropped me in the tub. At least this time he didn't burn me with the water.

"You're so fat!" he spat out.

I wanted to cover my body up as he stood over me in the tub. "Please not now," I cried, trying to bathe myself.

"What are you going to do with all this weight on you? You are so fat and ugly. You better be glad you have me because you'd never find someone else. You're just a big ole whale." He laughed and shook his head. "Ewww. You look so disgusting. Why you got to look so crazy?"

My tears were plentiful as he walked out of the bathroom still laughing at me. Listening to him I knew that he had absolutely nothing left for me. No matter how many times he apologized for his actions, it was clear that he simply didn't mean it. None of his seemingly endearing apologies ever came from his heart. I needed to get myself together. The way I saw it, life was about me and Trey now. Sitting in the tepid water, I prayed to myself. *Lord, help me to get my strength. Lord, please help me to find forgiveness in this horrible person I'm dealing with on a daily basis. Lord, I know you can change anything. Lord, please show me my next move. Just show me. Trey needs me and he loves me. My son is the only thing I have. Lord, I pray to you on this day to relieve me from all the pain and get me back on my feet. Amen.*

I knew a long time ago that J didn't love me anymore. I didn't even know if he was capable of loving anyone. Our marriage was already over before we even moved to Texas so I'm not surprised, but why did he have to be so hurtful to me? Why couldn't he just leave? I knew that I looked horrible, but what could I do? I began to wonder what I could do to make myself feel better. My self-esteem has been low for the longest and at some point I'd stopped feeling like a woman. I felt that I didn't have any worth. There I was, a huge very unattractive woman whom no man would probably ever want to look at. My husband hated me and despite my appearance I couldn't understand why?

"Stop it," I said to myself. There I was again thinking that it was all my fault. That obviously wasn't the case. I needed to stop making excuses for someone who didn't care about me and stop taking responsibility for his lack of good judgment and humanity. I needed to stop thinking about what J thought or what he liked, how he felt or what made him behave the way he did because it was not about him anymore.

I lay in the tub for almost two hours without realizing that he had left the house once again. He returned about three hours later. The water had grown ice cold and my skin was completely dried out. I was freezing. I couldn't believe that he'd just abandoned me that way.

"How dare you leave me in the tub for all this time?" I asked him as he sauntered into the bathroom as if he'd been there the whole time.

He was silent as he roughly grabbed me up causing a bruise to form on my arm right away. I looked into his eyes as I winced from the pain of his touch. There was nothing there but a sinister expression. I was looking at the devil live and in person. He dragged me to the bedroom and sat me on the bed.

"Can you bring me something to put on?" I asked him, thinking about all of the unpacked boxes.

"What the hell?" he complained. "It's not like you can fit anything no way."

So I settled upon one of his large t-shirts and nothing else.

The next morning at 6 AM he was preparing for work when I woke up. "Can you leave your cell phone?" I requested. "And pick up my other prescription?"

"I'm not giving you my phone," he stated.

"What!" I screamed at him. "I can't sit here for long hours every day and no form of communication. I need to be able to reach someone if something happens to me."

"I can't give you my phone," he insisted. "I'll be back around lunch time. You'll be fine."

"But what if I'm not?"

"That's why you should have stayed in the hospital." He exited the room and the house without another word and without leaving the phone.

I couldn't believe him. His gall just got worse and worse with each passing day. I was trying to keep calm because I knew that stress was the last thing I needed. But, around 10 AM, pain started to run through all of my body. I didn't know where it came from. My stomach started to feel really hot which was unusually odd to me. I looked at my belly underneath my shirt and saw a huge boil sticking out of my skin. In shock, I touched it to find that it was hot. Its coloring was black and blue at the same time.

I needed to use the bathroom. I got up too quickly and immediately fell. I was not able to keep my balance and was tired of constantly thudding to the ground. I crawled to the bathroom but could not get up on the toilet seat. I was in so much pain. I just sat there staring at the walls and trying to pray away the feeling of tormenting my body. About two hours later I heard the front door open. Within seconds, J entered the bathroom. From my awkward position I could see the look of disgust on his face.

Reluctantly, he picked me up off of the floor. "You need to get dressed," he told me. "I'm taking you back to the hospital."

Once again he took me to the military hospital but I already knew they weren't going to help me. The main hospital was only twenty minutes further out so I didn't understand why he didn't just take me there.

"I don't have time to drive you all the way to Temple Texas," he growled when asked.

"What is more important than me right now?"

"My job," he answered.

I didn't understand the problem. "So are you trying to tell me that if you tell them that your wife is seriously ill they're not gonna let you get off?"

"No. I'm the only one that is in charge of everything."

I nodded, not really caring to talk about it further. "I see!"

We arrived at the military hospital and shortly after they checked me in they called me up to the receptionist's desk to let me know that I would have to go back to K&T Hospital.

J threw his hands up in the air. "Well, I don't have the time to take you there," he spoke harshly to me. He turned to face the lady at the desk. "Can you guys call the paramedics for her?"

I felt so ashamed as I stood there listening to my husband work it out with the hospital staff to have me transported to K&T by ambulance. He didn't even bother to give me a proper goodbye before basically handing me off to them. Upon arriving at the ER, I was surprised to see how many people already knew me by my first name.

"Oh no, honey! What's the matter?" a familiar looking nurse asked me as she came over to handle my intake.

I pointed on the boil on the side of my stomach.

"Oh jeez!" she exclaimed, taking one look at it. "Um…I believe Dr. Xu is in the clinic so let's page him. I think it's best to have the doctor most familiar with you work with you, okay hun?"

Within no time, Dr. Xu came running into the room they'd placed me in. "Melissa, what is going on? What brings you back to us so quick?"

Again, I pointed to the gruesome boil on my stomach.

"Hmmm," he said during his examination. "There appears to be some kind of infection going on." He turned to look over at the nurse. "Let's take Melissa to the third floor." He looked back at me. "I'll see you in a little bit, Melissa."

I didn't realize that this visit would land me in the hospital for a whole month. While I was glad to be away from J, I also missed my son tremendously. It had been over half a year since I last saw him. By the time Dr. Xu and the hospital staff released me again, I couldn't wait any longer to lay eyes on my son. I demanded that J drive me to Louisiana that very same weekend. I was so happy to see my son. The moment he looked at me he started to cry. His tears brought on tears of my own. His vocabulary was picking up and his diction was so country sounding that it was hilarious. I wanted to pick him up and hold him in my arms so badly, but I couldn't. I wasn't yet well enough. I was surprised that Trey remembered me since I was clearly one hundred and fifty pounds heavier than before. I was able to sit him on my lap and from there he gave me the love I yearned for. He just kept on hugging me. I wanted to cry out of happiness!

From across the room my mother-in-law looked at me with a scared expression on her face. "Melissa, what did they do to you?"

I knew she was referring to the weight and my appearance. "It's the medicine they gave me," I explained. "It made me gain over one hundred and fifty pounds but I'll get rid of it quickly, believe me. How was little man behaving?" I asked to change the subject.

"He's been good. Just being a typical boy. You know how these boys are."

"Good," I replied, kissing Trey on both cheeks.

"He definitely loves to eat," Christine commented.

"Has J sent you any money at all while I was gone?"

She sucked her teeth. "Child, no!"

I wasn't surprised, but I felt so bad. I mean, this was his mother and she was doing us a huge favor by caring for our only child while I was hospitalized. Due to his carelessness, I felt obligated to do something to show my gratitude. I knew that she wasn't getting any support from anywhere for the other children she was tending to so I couldn't understand why J wouldn't even so much as provide the household with groceries if nothing else. She doesn't even have enough to take care herself, I thought, as I looked around at her modest accommodations and then at her tired demeanor.

"I really appreciate you, Ms. Christine," I said earnestly. "Let me do something for you. How about a makeover, huh? I could braid your hair up for you."

Her hand flew up to her head and the tattered pony tail hanging at her nape. "Yeah?" she asked.

I smiled. "Yeah."

So we went to the store to buy some hair in order to get the project started. I felt so much better knowing that I was putting a smile on her face. Back in her living room, I sat on the couch and she sat on the floor between my knees as I began braiding her salt and pepper hair.

"Melissa," Christine said softly about fifteen minutes into me braiding.

"Hmmm?"

"I know my son is not a good husband to you," she said. "And I'm sorry if I ever gave you the impression that I thought his behavior was okay. It's just that you two come from two completely different grounds."

"That never mattered to me," I told her. "From the beginning your son basically told me nothing but lies. He said that you all had a maid, he was an NFL Player, he was raised by his grandmother…Even though I realized it was all a lie, I still tried to be a good wife to him." I thought about it for a minute. "Why do you think he told me all of these lies, Mom?"

She sighed. "I can't explain it, dear."

It was a shame. Even his own mother couldn't figure him out. I wanted to unleash all of the anguish that was inside of me during that conversation. My marriage to J was over, but I just didn't have the guts to let my mother-in-law know. After finishing the last row of braids I was feeling very tired. I told Ms. Christine that I was going to lay down for a second. It was Mid-Summer in Louisiana and one hundred and three degrees outside but I was freezing. Laying on Ms. Christine's bed, I had two blankets yet still asked her for a third one.

"Melissa, it's burning up outside. What you need all these blankets for? You can't possibly be cold."

I looked at her and shrugged. My body was shivering and I was scared. Watching the way, I trembled and seemed to be turning colors, my mother-in-law started to scream. "Somebody please call 911!"

From the front of the house J and his uncle Tim, who was a police officer, came bounding into the room to see what the matter was. Ms. Christine insisted that they get me some medical attention right away. Everything became a blur and before I knew it I was back at the hick hospital in Louisiana that couldn't help me before.

"Why is this lady back here at our hospital?" the same, unhelpful doctor from before barked. "We simply cannot help her here. She hasn't got any help yet?"

The commotion in the exam room blended into a constant whining sound as my eyes fluttered and consciousness became nearly nonexistent. I was feeling extremely light and felt myself welcoming the feeling as a mechanism for blocking out all of the drama going on around me.

"Oh my God! I think we're losing her!" It was the last audible line that I could make out before the darkness took over.

***

"You haven't been taking your medicine as instructed," Dr. Xu stated. "That's why your body collapsed. Your body is depending on these meds. What were you thinking?"

I was back at K&T and Dr. Xu was giving me a scolding. I knew that he had a vested interest in my wellness, but the reason I did not take my meds was so that I could shed some of the pounds that I'd put on.

"I want to be skinny again," I told him. "Maybe then my husband will accept me and love me again. I'm tired of being fat."

The doctor shook his head. "Fat or skinny, if you plan on living you need to take your medicine. Your mother-in-law brought us your pill bottle and not one was missing since the prescription was filled at the pharmacy upon your release." He looked at me with disappointment in his eyes.

From that day forward I knew that the medicine was my lifesaver. I promised him that I wouldn't go without taking them again. I was tired of the whole ordeal and being shuffled from hospital to hospital. I was ready to try my hand at a more manageable lifestyle. Most importantly, I was ready to be back with my son.

***

I had to slowly but surely start motivating myself. The first thing I set my sights on was unpacking. Even though I'd been gone yet again for a few weeks, the house still looked the same. I began trying to make the house more of a home for Trey and I. J was never really a factor during this time. I took my medicine every day and started to move around as much as my body would allow me to. I was not able to do a lot, but every day I started to feel stronger and stronger.

It took me about three months to get back to looking almost like myself. My jeans started to fit again. I was so happy that I could not believe it. My husband didn't realize the transformation because he stayed out and would not come home most of the time. Whenever he was home he would just stay in the bedroom. I didn't care anymore as long as he didn't try to touch me in anyway.

One day while I was cleaning up I found a letter from the government. Apparently, J had received orders to depart to Iraq by the end of the month. I figured that it was my perfect chance to start my life over. I would have the ability to practice getting over him since he wouldn't be in my space.

When he got home from work that day he actually showed me the letter. Of course I acted like I had never seen it before in my life. "What's this?" I asked when he tossed the letter into my lap.

"Read it!" he encouraged.

So I read it as if it was my first time pouring over the words. "Oh wow! So they are going to ship you overseas. Wow!"

"Yup. And you won't be staying here?" he said shocking me.

"What do you mean by that?" My heart did flips. There was no way that Trey and I were going to deploy with him.

"I will pay for you a ticket to go back to Germany," he advised.

The thought was compelling but something was missing. "You mean me and my son, right?"

"No, just you."

J basically wanted me to leave and go back to Germany without my son.

"I'm not going anywhere without Trey," I told him. I considered the fact that he had my papers and still had ties to me. There was no way I was just going to fade away with him still holding the reigns. "No, I'm not going anywhere unless our divorce is final." I looked at him sternly. "I understand that our marriage is over so why don't we just kill it? No more games, J. Let's handle this like adults. If you don't want me in your life any more than just say goodbye to me and your son and we'll be gone. Give me back my documents and grant me a divorce. It's as simple as that."

Only it wasn't. J wasn't ready to let it go. The moment I encouraged him to go through with the divorce and to go ahead and send Trey and I both to Germany, he reneged on the idea. It was clear that he liked having the upper hand and divorcing me and setting us free would rob him of that. I'd done my best to make the house homely. I'd cleaned up, unpacked, put up the DVD player so that my son and I could at least watch movies. If he wasn't willing to send us both to Germany with divorce papers then he could just keep food and clean clothes on us and we'd be just fine. I assured him that I wouldn't give him any worries.

"Live your life and we'll live ours," I told him.

Later on that evening it dawned on him that he missed our son and decided to pick him up the next day. His abrupt softness made me thank God for wisdom and strength. After the proposition that I'd given him, I began to think that maybe he was finally coming to his senses. I could not be more excited about the idea of having my baby back with me.

When he woke up the morning he seemed to be in brighter spirits. “Good morning,” he told me. It was the first time in ages that he’d greeted me in such a way. “Wow. You look great.” He was finally noticing my weight loss as he looked at me in a tank top and sweat pants.

I was stunned. It was just too good to be true. I distinctly remembered all the times he’d made fun of me and called me ugly. “Don’t you think it’s a little too late for compliments?”

He grabbed my hands and looked me dead in my eyes. “Look, I want to have a serious talk about our marriage.”

Silly me, I sat down and listened to what he had to say about saving our marriage. I took in his whole speech about being lost and not having any clear direction as to how to be a good husband or father. I remained silent as he vowed to work harder on making us work out. I almost teared up when he mentioned praying for forgiveness of the way he’d treated me when I needed him the most. My little voice was telling me that clearly God has shown me time and time again that this man is not for me, but with nowhere to go or anyone to talk to about the matter, what else could I do? I figured that I might as well save my marriage. Who knew? Perhaps was really ready to change this time.

While I was thinking that he wanted to make our family work all he really wanted was sex. He apologized a million times about the things he did to me and found a million excuses for why he acted the way he did. I gave in to his cunningness and found myself allowing him to use my body for his own perverse pleasures. I figured that if we were going to make things work then I would truly have to forgive him and regard him as my husband the way that a wife should.

After an awkward sexual bout, J headed off to retrieve my son. My body wouldn't allow me to sit through that eight-hour drive so I waited at home patiently for them to return. I was so excited that I could hardly wait. The moment they walked through the front door together. I had a feeling deep inside of me that I couldn't describe. I was so happy and overjoyed that I did not know what to do with Trey first. Mommy's little man was back. My life seemed to be restored as I embraced my son.

I'd prepared tacos because it was the only meal that we had all of the ingredients for. "Are you hungry?" I asked Trey with a smile.

He nodded enthusiastically and I sent him on his way to wash his hands. As he went running up the hall screaming playfully, I actually saw a smile on my husband's face. It was the first time in a long time that I'd witnessed that beautiful grin. For a minute it felt like I had my family back. We didn't have much and our past was so shaky, but I felt that we could be on the path to better days. I asked God, "Are you showing me how this could be us again or are you still telling me to move on despite this one second of my husband not acting obnoxious?" I needed a clear sign.

~ Chapter 7~

Fed Up

"We think sometimes that poverty is only being hungry, naked and homeless. The poverty of being unwanted, unloved and uncared for is the greatest poverty." –Mother Theresa

J went from happy to controlling in a heartbeat. The moment I thought that maybe we were experiencing a breakthrough, his true personality came right into view.

"Where's my food?" he asked in a demanding tone. Gone was that bright smiled he'd just donned.

"It's almost finished," I replied breathlessly. I'd been on my feet quite a bit and I was starting to feel a little weak. I sat down on the living room couch to take a break as I waited for Trey to soar back into the room.

J had gone into the bedroom and scurried right back out with a sinister look in his eyes. "Come here for a second," he beckoned.

I gave him a questioning look. "What's the matter?"

"Nothing, just come in the room for a minute."

"I want to play with Trey for a minute and I still have to finish dinner, J," I complained.

He came closer to me. "I just want a quickie," he said in what I guess was supposed to be a seductive manner.

I shook my head. "No, we can't. Trey just got home and I'm really tired." I saw the flicker of anger in his eyes as his expression changed. Quickly, I apologized. "I'm sorry, baby. It's not that I don't want to, it's just that I'm not feeling very well. I just can't right now. And with the baby--"

"You're not worth a dime," he hissed, waving me off and cutting me short. "Who wants to live with a wife that he can't even have sex with!" he yelled.

I could hear Trey in his room playing with the toys I'd set out for him. I was glad that he hadn't returned to the living room to hear his father verbally abusing me. That was no kind of way to begin his first day back home. “Shhh! Lower your voice,” I begged J.

“This is my house! I don’t have to lower my voice!” he boomed. “Now where is my freaking food?”

I rose from the sofa and hurried to the kitchen. “Just let me make Tre’s plate and I’ll get yours,” I called over my shoulder.

Although I’d risen to get the food on the table, it still wasn’t good enough for J. He followed me into the kitchen. “No, make my plate now,” he demanded, taking a seat at the table.

Just when I thought the atmosphere has changed for a little bit he was back in his zone, bossing me around and speaking to me as if I was his maid and not his wife.

I continued preparing a small portion for my son. “Just give me a second,” I told my husband.

He banged his fist on the table just as Trey entered the kitchen, causing the little guy to jump. “I am the man in the house and the man of the house should receive his plate first!” he griped.

I was trying my best to ignore him. I motioned towards Trey with his plate in my hand. “Come on, baby. Come to the table.” I sat his plate down and tried to help him up into the booster seat I’d placed in a chair for him.

“Do you hear me?” J asked. “I am the man of this house and you gonna listen to me.” He suddenly rose from the table. “Matter-of-fact, you gonna give me some!”

I looked up at him like he was crazy as he glared at me.

“Put our son in his room,” he told me.

“J, please. The child is ready to eat. Let him eat first.” Although my mouth was pleading with him to just shut up and get over this rant he was on, my soul feared for the worst. I viewed my husband as the devil given all of the horrid things he’d done to me in the past, but considering his declaration of turning over a new leaf I hoped that he wouldn’t choose that moment to be violent towards me. He knew my medical condition was very bad. Why would he bother to come at me this way? I scooted our son up to the table and quickly tried to figure out what to do next. I gave up on prayers. It was clear that God wasn't hearing me. My brain flipped through scenarios as I backed away from the table towards the kitchen counter. I recalled that he hadn't locked the door earlier when they came in. Perhaps that was my way out.

"Put the boy in his room!" J repeated through clenched teeth."

I stared into his stone cold expression and swallowed hard. "Okay," I said softly. I grabbed Trey from his chair and carried him to his room as he whimpered out of longing for his dinner. I'm just going to run out of the door, I thought as I settled Trey in his room. I wasn't exactly sure of how I was going to accomplish that considering the fact that I was barely able to walk. I didn't want to leave him there but there was no way that I could run at all while carrying him given my condition. I kissed my son's forehead before exiting his bedroom. Softly, I pulled the door up behind me and peered down the hall towards the front door. It was now or never. I took a deep breath and before I could rethink the situation I high-tailed it for the door, grabbing my keys off of the hook beside it, snatching the door open before bolting outside and down the driveway. At some point I stopped and realized that I was just some ways down the street. I took both of my hands and pressed them against my stomach to take the pressure off as my chest heaved uncontrollably. I felt as if I was going to collapse right there on the asphalt. Pain shot through my back and my stomach was feeling like I had little bricks inside of it that were shaking as I began to somewhat speed walk away from my subdivision.

I was surprised that he didn't come after me. I guess he knew that I couldn't get far. The sun was going down. This is the first time I had ever been out of my house since returning from the hospital. I didn't know the area so I didn't know where to go. I considered knocking on someone's door or even just standing in the middle of the road screaming for help. The last thing I wanted to do was leave my son. I swear I didn't. I just couldn't stomach the idea of getting raped by my husband. I clutched my keys in my hands as I found myself walking down long street just miles away from my subdivision. It grew darker and darker. Tears rolled down my face and my body began to shiver. I was so scared and unsure of what to do. J often told me that if I ever told anyone what went on in our home that he would kill me. Looking around the dark empty streets I felt as if I was going to die anyway.

"Where are you going?" I asked myself out loud. "Where are you walking to, Melissa?" All sorts of things started to run through my mind. *Why don't you just walk into a car and get hit hard enough that you don't have to take this pain anymore?* But I couldn't do it for the same reason that I didn't want to be killed by my husband--I loved life too much. I was simply tired of the way my life was going. Spotting a bench up ahead, I stopped and sat down. I didn't know where to go from there. It was now completely dark outside. I couldn't help but to start crying. "Can somebody help me?" I screamed through my troubled sobs. "JESUS!" I yelled for the savior but I still wasn't convinced that he was paying my struggles any attention. I started crying even louder. I knew that no one was hearing my cries.

Defeated, I got up and slowly walked back to the house. As I opened the door J was sitting on the couch waiting for me. My heart plummeted the moment our eyes met. He got up and started to beat on me as if I was a thief that had just attempted to rob him of his money. I didn't even bother to object at this point. I just took the beating. Once he was finished, he got off of me, walked two steps away from my crumbled over body, and then turned back around to spit in my bruised face. I waited until I no longer heard him moving about in the bedroom before I got up off of the floor, picked up my clothes that he'd torn from my body, and tried to lie down on the couch. My legs were sore I did not know if I should cry or laugh. They always say that God wouldn't put you through anything that you aren't able to handle. I wondered how much more of this I supposed to be able to handle before God finally said, "Enough!"

Following this huge fight, J packed up about three bags. I could only thank God. He was finally leaving. Since he packed his bags I knew he wasn't coming back anytime soon. J didn't leave us any money when he took off so I had to be really careful with how I prepared our meals. But, as long as my son had what he needed I was good. With J gone, I woke up my son every morning while it was still cool outside so that we could take a walk. I was no longer afraid to come out of the door. I needed to exercise my muscles and get the feeling back in my legs.

One morning as we came home from our walk I heard someone say, "I did not know someone was living next to me. Hey handsome little boy!"

I had on my sunglasses to cover up my bruises. Not knowing who the lady was, I rushed my son back inside of the house. If she was my neighbor, I wondered how come she'd never heard my screams or cries for help. Trey and I got washed up and had just laid down for a nap when I heard a knock at the door. I hesitated for a second. No one ever came to our house. After the second round of knocking I tiptoed to the window and peeked out to see who was invading my space. It was the same lady. I didn't feel like talking and going through the series of questions that nosy neighbors ask so I didn't go to the door. I saw her leave a note and wondered what it was that she could possibly want.

From looking at her I guesstimated that we were around the same age. Sweat dripped into my eye from my forehead as I tore myself away from the window. Our house was as hot as a sauna. That was another reason why I hadn't felt inclined to invite the woman in. I didn't want to be embarrassed. I waited until I was sure that she'd returned to her own home before cracking the door and snatching down the note she'd left for me. Hurriedly, my eyes poured over her words.

Call me. I'd love to get to know you and your son better!

My nose wrinkled up. I thought it was strange that she would be so cordial to people she'd only seen in passing for two minutes, but I figured that it might be a good thing. I didn't have a home phone or a cell phone so I couldn't call her back. I just had to wait until the next time we ran into her in order to respond to her invitation.

I didn't have to wait long. Later in the day, as Trey and I were outside playing with his ball, she pulled up in her driveway. Ecstatically, she waved to us as she got out of the car. "Hey how are you guys!" She stood a safe distance between her yard and mine. "Hey, I'm Melanie."

I smiled politely. "Hi, Melanie"

"And who is this handsome fella of yours?" she asked, looking over at my son as he continued playing with his ball.

“His name is Trey,” I answered, beaming proudly at my little man.

“Why don’t you guys come over? We can have a snack or something and get to know one another.”

“Umm…okay,” I said hesitatingly. “Umm… let me just get him cleaned up.”

She smiled at me and turned to retrieve her packages from her car.

I took Trey inside and washed him up before cautiously heading over to Melanie’s. I hoped that my appearance didn’t alarm her given the healing bruises on my face and extremities. Walking into her house we were met by an arctic cold blast. It felt really good compared to the sweltering heat that we were accustomed to. I hadn’t been in air conditioning in so long that I almost forgot how great it felt.

Melanie wasted no time in chatting. She started to tell me that she lived there all by herself and that her husband was a contactor overseas. “I had no idea that a female lived next door,” she gushed excitedly as she handed me a glass of lemonade. “I’m used to only seeing a guy pull up.”

The first thought that ran through my mind was that my husband was trying to flirt with her.

“Is he your husband?”

“Yes,” I replied.

“He’s a very nice guy.”

I wanted to laugh. “Of course,” I replied sarcastically in a hushed tone.

During our visit she told me that she was from the Virgin Island but grew up in Texas. I learned that her mother ran a daycare in the city also.

“If you ever feel like taking a break my mom won’t mind keeping him,” Melanie offered.

I thought that was so nice of her. She was very kind and the entire visit seemed to be going really well until she asked me to go to the mall with her.

“Umm…I’m not really into shopping malls,” I lied. The thought of window shopping, because the truth was I had no money, and being scrutinized by a total stranger as I tried stuff on was not appealing to me.

"Well, what *do* you like to do?" she asked considerately.

I shrugged. "I don't know. I'm really a homebody. Watching movies, cooking…"

"I see," she replied with a smile. She took a look at Trey who was eyeing her quietly. "How about we go out and get a milkshake?" she asked. "My treat."

I didn't want to accept any charity but Trey's eyes glazed over with excitement at the sound of a field trip and the promise of a treat. So, I agreed and we all filed into her car to drive to the nearest Dairy Queen.

The moment his nose got a whiff of the fast food around us, my son went crazy. "Fries, Ma! Fries!" he yelled out.

Immediately, I regretted the decision to make the trip. I couldn't get mad at Trey though. It wasn't his fault that his mommy didn't have any money to buy him food.

“Are you guys hungry?” Melanie asked. “We could do lunch before the milkshake.”

“No, no. We’re fine,” I said with a quick smile.

“Fries, Mama!” Trey repeated.

I felt my face become flush with embarrassment.

“Are you sure?” Melanie asked. “I don’t mind really.”

I looked at the pitiful expression on my son’s face. “Well, maybe just for Tre. I’m fine. I would get it myself but we were only planning to make a quick visit to your place so I didn’t grab my wallet and--” I began to explain.

Melanie silenced me with a wave. “Oh, girl. It’s okay. I don’t mind. I told you it was my treat.” She grabbed Trey’s hand and they approached the counter to order their food.

I liked seeing my son enjoying himself, even though it wasn’t me who had placed the smile upon his face. Unable to resist and feeling the rumbling of my tummy, I stole two French fries from my son. I savored each one. They tasted like the best food I'd ever had in my life.

After that Melanie and I became great friends. Full days would sail by without me noticing as we hung out in the coolness of her home. At some point we went to visit her mom's daycare and Trey loved it. He hadn't been around any kids since leaving his grandmother's house. Seeing the way, he interacted with the children, Melanie's mom, Ms. Vera, offered for him to stay.

"Why don't you two go enjoy the afternoon and let this baby stay here and play," Ms. Vera insisted. "Where does he usually go to day care?"

I cleared my throat. "He uh…he doesn't. He stays home with me. I'm a stay at home mom."

"Oh I see. Well, even stay at home moms get tired so bring him on over here sometime and let him play with the other children."

I was touched by her generosity. "Thank you. I'll do that." I knew that I didn't have any money to pay for Ms. Vera's services, but it felt good knowing that I had somewhere I could take him if ever I needed to and was able to.

I really liked Melanie and her mother. It felt good to know that there were still kind people in the world, despite the monster I'd been stuck with for so long.

***

"Let's go out," Melanie suggested.

It was around 8 PM and we were hanging out at her mother's house. My son was getting tired and I wasn't really feeling the idea of partaking in the nightlife.

"Um, I really should be getting back home," I told Melanie.

"Why? You expecting a call from your husband?" she questioned.

That was the last thing I was expecting. He hadn't come by to check on our son in over a week which was fine with me.

"No. It's just that Tre's sleepy and I should get him to bed."

"My mom can keep him," Melanie offered. "You know she doesn't mind."

I looked down at my jeans and white wife beater, some of the only clothes that I had which weren't ruin from being ripped by J or destroyed during our moves. "I don't really have any clothes to go out."

"That's okay! We can head to the mall. You're a size small so you should be able to find something cute for cheap."

I gave a skeptical look.

"I got you, girl," she assured me. "But we gotta go before the mall closes."

Before I knew it we were running through the mall and piecing together an outfit that I would feel comfortable in. Soon after we were walking into a club downtown. As it turned out, neither of us were big clubbers. But, Melanie was missing her husband and wanted to get out so there we were. I was surprised when no one asked for our IDs upon admission. The music was blasting and I was vaguely reminded of the days when my friends and I use to hit up our favorite spot on the weekends. Seeing all the people around me I became self-conscious. Although my clothes looked alright, I had on no makeup. I could remember a time when I would never dare to leave the house without makeup on. I thanked God at the moment that it was dark inside of the club.

As I walked past the bar I heard someone screaming out loud Securitas. I just kept on walking and paid it no mind. As I sat down at the bar the call was closer.

"Securitas!"

I looked around but all I saw were a few guys making their way over to the bar. Taking a closer look at the face of the man smiling hard and staring at me, I couldn't belief my eyes. It was one of my homeboys that used to be stationed in Germany. He was just as surprised to see me sitting there. Glancing around once more I noticed quite a few faces of soldiers that used to be stationed in Germany.

"What are you doing here?" TeTe asked me.

"I could ask you the same question," I responded.

We tried to catch up over the blare of the music, but eventually I just told him to write his number down so that I could call him.

"What happened to you?" he asked me as he scribbled his number on a napkin? "You're still beautiful but you look so different."

"Too much to tell in a club," I replied honestly.

I had a good time that night. It felt good to be out of the house and around people who weren't trying to hurt me. As we left the club I remembered that we needed to pick up my son from Melanie's mom's house.

"I'm sure he's asleep," she said. "We can pick him up in the morning."

I knew that she was tired, but there was no way that I was leaving my baby there until the morning. It was hard enough for me to agree to let him out of my sight long enough to enjoy the club. "If it's not too much trouble, I just really would like to get him now. Besides, I don't even have any money to pay your mom."

"That's okay. She doesn't mind."

"Melanie, really…I'd really rather not leave him."

She nodded her understanding and we proceeded to her mother's house. An hour later when I opened my front door, I thanked God that J wasn't there. As I put my son to bed I thought about TeTe. I wanted to call him so bad to let him know about the mess I'd gotten myself into. I wanted to ask him to help me get in touch with someone on the military base who could get me away from my husband. Standing in my home in the still of the night I realized that we were out of everything. I desperately needed someone to help me turn this situation around.

***

I needed a phone ASAP. All night I could not sleep. I rushed over to Melanie's house as soon as the sun came up. "I need a phone," I told her. "It's important!"

Half asleep, she trotted to her living room and handed me her cell phone. "Just bring it back later," she said while yawning.

"No way. It'll be quick." While dialing TeTe's number I saw that Melanie actually had a house phone. "Um, are you able to make overseas calls on your house phone?" I asked.

"Of course. That's how I talk to my husband every day. It's a flat rate."

"May I use that phone instead?" I decided that it was time to call my mother.

"Yes, honey! Now please…please, let me sleep." She trudged back to her bedroom leaving me alone to make my call.

I felt bad for waking her up but I was appreciative for the opportunity to call my mother. I waited patiently for the line to connect.

"Hello?" her voice answered uncertainly.

I smiled from ear to ear. "Hi, Mom. It's me. I only have a few minutes."

"Melissa? Baby, are you alright?"

"I need money, Mom," I blurted out honestly. "If you can please help me."

"Yes, yes of course!"

"Take down my address, okay?"

"Okay, hold on…let me get a pen…okay, what is it?"

I hurriedly gave the address before promising to call again soon. "I love you, Mom. And thank you!"

"Love you too, Baby!"

About a week later the letter from my mother arrived with $150 in it. I was the happiest person in the world. I was tired of mooching off of Melanie and eating up her food every day. I was glad for the resources to take care of my own son and myself for a change.

***

I knew my follow up appointment with my Dr. Xu was coming up. Melanie offered to watch Trey but I still needed a ride to my appointment. With no other options, I called TeTe. TeTe told me that he had to work and that he lived an hour away, but without a doubt he also said he'd take me anyway. Despite me begging him not to compromise his job for me, he assured me that my health was far more important. From that day forth I would forever be grateful for TeTe for coming to my aid. For him the word 'can't' just didn't exist.

Sitting in the waiting room at the doctor's office listening for my name to be called, I noticed a lady staring at me. I became uncomfortable with her stares and tried to turn away from her.

"Excuse me, sweetheart," she said, coming over to me. "How are you? My name is Eight."

What a peculiar name, I thought. "I'm fine, Ma'am. Did you need something?" The way she looked at me had me unnerved.

"Have you ever modeled before?" She couldn't be serious!

"Huh?"

"Like print ads or commercials" she explained.

"Umm…Yes," I answered shyly. "I was a model a long time ago." It was the truth. Before I'd fallen into the pit of hell that I called my marriage, back when I lived a stress-free life in Germany I'd had some modeling experience. "Why?"

"I own a modeling agency right here in Texas and I would love for you to be a part of my Agency."

"Really?" I was astonished.

"Oh yes, Ma'am!" She handed me her business card. "You be sure to give me a call soon, honey."

I looked at the card and smiled nervously. "Thank you, Ma'am. I really appreciate it."

She gave me a huge smile followed by an even bigger hug. "You're beautiful," she complimented me as she pulled back and took a final look at me. "Simply beautiful. Now, you make sure you use this card."

I nodded but remained silent. I knew that the lady could feel my pending rejection. I wasn't going to call her. I couldn't. The confident, outgoing, social, kindhearted person that once was me was gone. I appreciated her compliments and her kindness and in some way it did work to boost my spirits just a bit.

But, the truth of the matter was that I just didn't have the drive to be a model any longer.

Soon after, my name was called for my appointment.

"Melissa, you look great!" Dr. Xu exclaimed the moment he met me in the examination room. "What have you been doing."

I shook my head and shrugged. "I'm just trying to get back to my old self, Doc. I feel a lot better. I'm moving around a whole lot more…Just taking it one day at a time."

"Great! You're doing great!" he gushed. Dr. Xu prescribed me some more meds to help maintain my immune system and then I was out of the door.

Although TeTe had dropped me off, I took the bus back home. During the ride home I couldn't get the lady from the waiting room out of my head. She had me feeling a twinge of confidence that I hadn't experienced in a while. I was starting to think that maybe she was heaven sent.

Since I didn't have a phone at my house, I got off of the bus one stop early so that I could use a payphone at the corner store. Pulling out the card that the woman had given me, I nervously dialed the number. The line was picked up by a perky voice that made me stare hard at the glass of the phone booth while gripping the receiver tightly.

"May I speak with Eight please?" I asked timidly.

"Hello, this is Eight," the woman responded.

"Hello, Ma'am! My name is Melissa and I met you earlier today," I began to explain.

"Yes, yes! Hello, Darling! I knew you were going to call. I just felt it in my spirit."

"Uh…yes, well, I would like to get some more info on how I can be a part of your agency."

"I'm out and about on errands but is it possible for you to swing by my house instead of the office?"

"I don't really have transportation," I told her. "And I have a son so…"

"What's your address?"

I rattled it off for her in a hopeful tone.

"Okay, I'll meet you at your place in a couple of hours and then we'll have our meeting at my house. Fair enough?" she asked.

"Yes, that's great!"

"Okay, dear. See you then."

About two hours later she pulled up in my driveway. As it turned out, she only lived about ten minutes away from me. I quickly piled myself and Trey into the car and she whisked us off to her home. Her house was absolutely gorgeous. There were exquisite photos of her everywhere.

"I used to model myself," Eight explained to me as she watched me gawking at her life-sized portraits. "But, it was always my dream to have my own agency." She lingered for a moment as if reminiscing on her heydays and then sprung right into work mode. "So, are you ready to commit to a modeling career one hundred percent, Melissa?" she asked.

I considered the question and the alternative. I had nothing else going on for me. The only option that seemed to be on the table was the one that she was offering. “Yes,” I told her. “I’m ready.”

She smiled at me confidently. “Well then let’s get to it.” She pulled out an expensive camera and motioned me towards a photo set up on the other side of the room.

I hadn’t been in front of the camera in a long time. Living in that moment, I felt revived. Eight inspired me with her positive energy and constant affirmations. Despite the appreciation I had for what she was doing for me, my mind continued to travel to the reality of my life. I knew that once I left her environment, filled with beautiful pictures, air conditioning, and grandeur, that I would be forced to return to my shamble of a home. I questioned if I really deserved this opportunity.

Upon leaving Eight’s house, I had her drop us at that same payphone I’d gone to in order to call her. The moment she pulled off, I picked up the phone, inserted the necessary coins and dialed my sister Charlene’s number. I needed my family right now. The moment she answered, I broke out into tears.

"Hello?" Charlene called out into the phone at the sound of my sobbing. "Hello?"

"Charlene, it's me…Melissa..." I couldn't control my crying. "Sis, please help me. Please.

"What? Wait a minute, Melissa. Hold on. What's going on? You have to stop crying."

"Please just get me away from here. I can't take it any longer." I realized that my sister had no clue as to the hell I'd been suffering from all of this time. "I know this is short notice, but I really need to go."

"Okay, okay. Where are you? What happened, honey?"

I was running out of talk-time and Trey was growing tired. "I'm at a payphone," I explained. "And I don't really have time to get into the whole thing. But I really need your help. I really need to leave Texas, Charlene."

Sensing my urgency, she abandoned her questions. "Okay, sweetie. Is there a Greyhound station near you?"

"A what?" I was confused.

"A Greyhound bus station. They go all over the U.S."

I looked around frantically, feeling my chance to escape slipping away from me. "I-I-I don't know."

"Find out where the nearest one is and I'll get you a ticket to Atlanta."

Beep, beep.

Just as she made the last statement our call ended and I was out of money. I hung up the receiver, wiped my tears, and grabbed my baby. I was determined to change our situation then and there. I was not about to sit in that house waiting for J to come back and abuse me some more. I was done with it. Returning to my street I noticed that Melanie's car wasn't in her driveway. I needed help and I simply couldn't wait to see when she would return. Taking my chances, I headed over to my other neighbor's house. I'd never spoken to them before and had never even seen them in person. But, I was familiar with the car that rested in their driveway and I knew by the sight of it that someone was home.

I knocked on my neighbor's door and waited for a moment. Soon, an elder lady opened up the door.

"Hi, Ma'am. I'm Melissa, your neighbor," I explained.

The lady looked at me in surprise. "Why, I never knew that a lady was staying next to me. What can I do for you, sweetie? Are you the new boo?" she inquired with a sly smile.

I shook my head. "Um, no Ma'am. I am the wife."

"The Wife?" She was clearly confused. "Okay, are you talking about you're my neighbor to the left or to the right?"

I sighed. "To the right, Ma'am."

Her eyebrow rose in suspicion. "But the gentleman moved here about a year ago and told me that he was a single dad."

I wasn't shocked. "He's not the most honest person. But, can you tell me if there's a Greyhound bus station nearby?"

"Yes, actually there's one in downtown Killeen. About twenty minutes away. You going away?" She sure was nosey.

"Yes Ma'am," I replied confidently. "I'm leaving today." I glanced over at her car in the driveway. "Do you mind taking me and my son there please? I hate to impose but it's kind of an emergency."

She gave me a skeptical look. "Are you coming back?"

I sensed that she had some kind of loyalty to J and didn't want to mess up my chances of getting assistance. "Oh of course. I'm only going to be gone for a couple of days. Well, my son and I that is."

She slowly nodded. "Okay. Sure. It's no problem at all."

I was dancing for joy on the inside. "Okay, let me just grab our things and we'll be ready to go." I hurried into my house and filled Trey's bag with the little bit of juice that we had left, diapers, and wipes. I needed nothing for myself out of this house that was never really a home.

The moment the lady dropped us off at the station I cried out of happiness. I was finally one step closer to freedom. I hugged my son tight and went inside to retrieve the ticket that Charlene had purchased for me. Within thirty minutes the bus arrived and we filed onto it with the rest of the passengers. Snuggled down in the seat with Trey in my lap, I stared out of window. I watched as the bus pulled off and we began to leave it all behind. Goodbye Killen, Texas! Goodbye J! Goodbye old life!

~ Chapter 8~
Back-tracking

"Life can only be understood backwards; but it must be lived forwards." –Soren Kierkegaard

Fresh air! Life was just like that the moment I entered my sister's home. I felt free. There was no more pressure to keep my mouth closed in order to diffuse drama, no fear of being smacked out of the blue, and no feelings of contempt for the other adult in the house with me. Hundreds of miles separated me from that which had worked to help my self-esteem plummet. Like Terry McMillian had penned, I experienced an epic moment as the scent of lilac and washing powder mixed with a hint of freshly fried chicken assaulted my nose: I EXHALED. Even Trey seemed to be more at ease. I knew that children had a way of sensing when things were wrong. They were like ultra-absorbent sponges, soaking up everything going on in their environment. It was all the more reason why I desperately had to break free of the hold that J had on me. Because I was so certain that Trey's spirit had been tormented by the turmoil going on around him, I could tell that he now realized that our situation had changed. We were emancipated from the perils of domestic violence. Or so we thought.

No sooner than I'd sunken into the plushness of Charlene's couch, her phone rang. We were watching an episode of a far-fetched reality show, enjoying the luxury of just doing nothing. Trey was sitting on the floor near my feet entertaining himself with a plush toy that Charlene had given him. She reached over to grab the cordless phone from the end table to her right. She pressed the TALK button and answered while still staring at the television screen.

"Hello?"

A few seconds too long passed and a chill traveled down my spine. I looked over to see her staring at me with a shell-shocked expression. Her mouth wasn't moving but her facial expression and body language were speaking volumes. As she listened with her teeth gritted and from hearing the rise and fall of a male's voice I knew that it was him. I shook my head, partly out of shock that he'd been wise enough to find me there and partly in a desperate plea for her to tell him that I wasn't there.

"I don't know about all of that and I don't think I really want to be involved in it," Charlene said.

Too late, I thought. There was no chance of lying to him now and saying that I wasn't there. Obviously, he knew me well enough to know that I'd run to Atlanta and following my sister's proclamation he certainly knew that his assumption was correct. Moreover, I hadn't fully disclosed to Charlene what my home life was like. Now here she was getting an earful from my husband and getting a tiny glimpse of the type of hell I'd been enduring.

Quickly, I jumped up before J could say anything further to send my sister's tongue into overdrive. "It's okay," I told her. "It's okay. I've got it." I grabbed the phone out of her hand and looked quickly down at my baby's saddened expression as I walked out of the living room to take the call that had me trembling. Even across the distance and phone lines that separated us, J still had me completely shook. "Hello?"

"Who do you think you are?" he asked me. "You think you can take my son away from me and I'm not gonna do anything? Are you crazy? Don't you know that I'll kill you?"

I was sure that he meant it. I couldn't get a word in edgewise and I knew that if I did manage to say something that it would only infuriate him further. As he continued to berate me I had visions of him making his way from Texas to Georgia to severely punish me for running away. I was disappointed in myself for bringing my drama to my sister's house knowing full well how crazy and dangerous J was. There was no telling what he'd do to me or the chaos that would go down should he actually touch down in Atlanta and show up on Charlene's doorstep. I didn't want that to happen, but I didn't know what to do in order to save myself and Trey.

"I'm only going to tell you this once," he warned me in a thunderous tone. "I'm giving you one week to get yourself together and bring my son back home. Think I'm playing with you if you want, but if ya ass ain't here I promise you I'll come there and kill you."

The line went dead. I stared at the phone and quickly weighed my options. As I clicked off of the line, I bit down on my bottom lip. I believed him. I believed that if I didn't make my way back to Texas that he'd make good on his promise and I'd be dead. Slowly, I returned to the living room where Charlene was awaiting some explanation for the awkward phone call.

"Everything's fine," I told her. "No worries."

Her face let me know that she knew I was lying. "No worries? Then why do you look like the world's coming to an end?"

I wanted to tell her that it was because I felt as if the world really was ending, but I knew that I couldn't do that. I couldn't unleash my burdens on her. "No, just thinking about some things that I need to take care of when I get back. I don't know…after being sick it's just been so hard for me to get back in the swing of things, you know?" I gripped the phone tightly. "And J…he just wants me to come home so that we can figure it all out together, you know?

Men." I laughed it off. "He acts like he doesn't know how to survive without me being there."

Charlene nodded her understanding. "I know what you mean, girl. These men are like babies sometimes. They need you to be their mama, their accountants, their secretaries, their maids. Everything."

We shared a laugh although truthfully I was dying on the inside. Maybe Charlene's husband needed her in that way but I knew that my husband only wanted to control me. He could care less about having me around to be loving and nurturing. Despite my better judgement, my fear was in high gear and I knew that I would have to leave my family and return to the monster I'd married in order to keep everyone that I loved safe. Over the duration of the following week, I felt horrible knowing that I was such a burden to my sister. Just taking up more space in her home, eating her food, and running up her utility bills I felt out of place. I had nothing therefore I had no way of contributing to her household. How was I supposed to go on like that? My family was all very good natured about it. My sister Denise even came back to pick up

Trey a couple of times to take him to daycare with her son so that I could get some rest. They wanted me there, I could sense it, but I also knew that I was disrupting their regular lives by having them all take care of me and my son.

By the middle of the next week, I knew that I had to make a move. I kept running scenarios in my mind for how to get back home since I had no money. I was afraid to ask Charlene since she'd been so kind to pay for my bus tickets there and put Trey and I up in her home. I didn't want to alarm any of my family members about the troubles I was facing back home so I was hesitant to say anything at all to any of them. As I sat in the guest room of my sister's house racking my brain for solutions, I was startled by the ringing of the phone. She was at work and the only ones in the house at the time were me and Trey. Nervously, I answered for fear that it was J calling to reiterate his threat.

"Hello?" The shakiness of my tone was noticeable.

"Hello? Melissa?" the male's voice rang in my ear.

I was clueless. It wasn't J, of that I was certain, but I wasn't sure whether it was someone calling on his behalf or if maybe it was some family member that I hadn't yet visited with since being in town.

"This is Koby Michaels," he announced himself. "I ran into one of your sisters today and she told me you were in town. She gave me this number. You remember me don't you?"

I did indeed remember my old friend and immediately felt that it was a mighty small world that he'd be all the way here in Georgia. "Hi, Koby. Yes, yes, I remember you. It's good to hear from you."

"Likewise. Look, I was out here visiting some family in Augusta, just stopped through Atlanta to check on some property that I own. I'm on my way back to Texas tomorrow but I was wondering if I could come by and see you before I leave out."

Instantly, a light bulb went off in my head. It was as if the universe had brought Koby to me to help solve my problem. All I heard was the word Texas and I immediately knew that soon I'd be back with J facing God knows what kind of hell all in the name of keeping my son safe and saving my own life. "Sure," I told Koby as I repositioned myself on my bed. "But um, funny that you should mentioned heading out to Texas. You know, I'm actually a Texan…" I paused for a moment. "Do you think it would be a problem for me and my son to ride back with you?"

Koby let out a nervous laugh. "Well, umm…I wasn't expecting any passengers. I mean, I don't have a problem with it but I'm driving a two seater so I don't know how comfortable that would be for you and your son."

I was too close avoiding being murdered by J's hand to let this set me back. "No, no, it's okay. Really. My baby's still small and I'm sure if you're driving the speed limit then we'll have nothing to worry about."

"Are you sure? That's a rather long drive, Melissa."

"I'm sure," I told him. "We'll be fine."

So it was settled. Koby agreed to take us back with him and I quickly prepared to say goodbye to my family. My sisters had been kind enough to buy Trey new clothes and diapers that they insisted we take back with us seeing as though we'd shown up with nothing. Koby hadn't been lying. There was little to no space for our extra belongings but we somehow made it work. Trey sat between my legs, clinging to me for dear life, as I sat on top of our bags with my head practically poking out of the sun roof of the limited edition Firebird. I felt like a giraffe as I sat upright for hours, trying not to fidget and make Trey any more uncomfortable than he already was.

"So, I'm sure your husband's anxious for you to get home," Koby said to me three hours into our drive after Trey had fallen asleep.

We'd had a lot of meaningless conversations prior to that as well as a lot of catch-up type of discussions. During the process, I'd mentioned that I was married but he'd already gotten that tidbit of information prior to calling me up the day before.

"Oh…yeah," I lied. "That's why I jumped on the opportunity to come back out with you."

"If you were my wife and I missed you I would have come to get you myself."

The sentiment was sweet. I'd always known that Koby had a crush on me but growing up he'd never acted on it. Now, I was stuck in a situation that even I didn't understand so I knew that I had no business concerning myself with the feelings of another man or getting my own feelings invested for that matter.

"Well, I thought it would be good to surprise him," I said. "He works so much and I know he's so tired. I'm sure he would have come for us himself but I just didn't want to put any more on him."

"Hmmm."

I could tell that Koby wasn't fully buying my story and I didn't blame him. I could hear myself and there wasn't a convincing syllable in the words that I'd spoken. Still, I couldn't disclose my truth and risk mine or Trey's life any more than I already had. I was sure that J was sitting around fuming and plotting exactly how he would end my life if I didn't show up at home soon. The thought of returning to him and the ungodly living situation he held me captive in made my stomach turn. A part of me wanted to jump out of the car with Trey and run in the opposite direction, but it was too late to turn back now. I was steadily moving in a direction back towards a man whom I knew didn't love me, a man that I knew would ultimately cause me more bodily harm upon my return. I was scared out of my mind but I was even more afraid of the consequences should I not return home

By the time Koby dropped us off at the home that I dreaded, it was late night. I was surprised that J wasn't standing guard staring out of the window anticipating my return. It alarmed me that he didn't bother to peep out if only to see who was pulling up in his driveway and then I realized the blessing in his negligence. It was much better this way. I didn't want

J to start any trouble with Koby who was only being a good friend by dropping Trey and me off in the first place. With mixed feelings, I slid from the mountain of bags with Koby's assistance and juggled a sluggish Trey in my arms.

"I'll take your things to the porch," Koby offered.

I held my breath as he worked and prayed that J didn't choose that moment to swing open the front door and make a scene. Nothing happened. Koby returned to the passenger side of his car where I was still standing and smiled at me.

"Well, that's all of it," he announced.

I smiled and tried to look strong as my body and spirit pleaded with him to see past the façade and beg me to get back into the car. "Thanks so much. I appreciate your help. It was extremely kind of you."

"I don't mind it at all. You two take care and don't be a stranger okay?"

"I won't. I'll call you soon to see how you are."

"Sounds good."

I watched as Koby backed out of the driveway and pulled out of our lives. That feeling of being alone in turmoil became my reality once more. As I turned to face my house I mused over how beautiful it actually was on the outside even in the darkness of night. If only the rest of the world knew the ugliness of the environment within the home. As I walked to the front door I notice that there were no lights on inside at all. My body began to shiver with fear and from the chill of the night air. I couldn't believe that I was submitting to the hell that I'd so valiantly escaped from, but there I was ringing the doorbell to be let in and welcomed back to the insanity. Receiving no response to my constant pushing of the doorbell, I wandered around to the back of the house to see if any lights were on in the far rooms of our home. There was no glow coming from any of the windows. I stared at the stillness of our backyard and for a moment I envisioned what it would be like to be a normal family making the most of the blessing this home should have been.

It was clear that J wasn't home. I could only imagine where he was at this time of the night as Trey and I sat out in the cool of night waiting for him. With nowhere else to go and no other resource because I didn't have a key to the house, Trey and I found a spot on the grass in the backyard and clung to one another. It was nearly two in the morning. I rocked Trey to sleep and as he snored lightly I went over and over my options in my head. I still had time to rise and walk away from it all but now that I'd come this far where was I going to go with no resources to get me there? I couldn't very well call my sister up again with the same request after abruptly bidding her and the others farewell to come home. Finally, around 4 A.M. in the morning, I heard the sound of the garage door rising. I hurriedly awakened Trey and pulled him in a bad dash to the front door so that his father would let us in.

As we rounded the corner I could see that J was already out of his car. He'd just hit the button next to the door leading into the house as he fumbled to unlock the bottom lock of the door. I was panting, half tired out from running and have exasperated to be looking at the man who I'd learned to loathe.

"Wait!" I called out, holding up my hands and leaning over in exhaustion.

J heard my frantic cry and quickly turned around. His eyes narrowed to slits as he focused on the sight of our figures standing just a few feet away in the driveway as the garage door lowered. Immediately, he pressed the button again and the garage door reversed its direction. I tried to control my breathing and brace myself as J walked towards us. I just knew that he could hear my heart thudding loudly through my chest. Like an animal, I knew that he had detected the fear that lingered within me. I bit my bottom lip as I blinked profusely while looking at his emotionless face. When he came to a stop just in front of us my soul began to weep and I was angry with myself for being weak enough to return to him.

"Come here, Trey," he said, lowering his eyes to meet those of our son. "Come give your daddy a hug."

Trey was motionless. He looked up at me as if to ask whether or not it was okay. I understood his hesitation; he was conscious of his father's previous temperament and like me he wasn't sure what to expect.

J held his arms out. "Come on, son."

Trey hesitated a second longer but then took three steps to fall into his father's embrace. J scooped him up, took a step forward, and then turned his back to me. For a moment, I thought he was going to leave me standing there in the driveway looking helpless as he carried my son away from me. I was grateful that he hadn't struck me right then at the break of day but I was not about to let him tear my heart into shreds by taking my child from me. Before I could voice my concerns, he surprised me even more by reaching back and throwing his arm around my shoulders. I winced at his touch, unused to him being affectionate or so much as cordial these days.

"Come on in the house," he instructed. His tone was neutral and I was unsure of how to read it or him.

Once inside, J locked the door and looked over Trey as if he was expecting him to see if anything was wrong. I was a good mother so I knew that he wouldn't find nary a scratch on Trey. In fact, I thought that it was ironic of him to go through such measures considering that he was the dangerous one that couldn't be trusted. But, I said nothing. I simply looked around the house noticing that not much had changed since I'd decided to vacate.

"Dad's exhausted," J said to Trey. "Are you tired, son?"

Trey nodded.

"Let's say we watch some cartoons and take a nap. That sound good?"

Trey nodded again.

J looked over at me and I found myself holding my breath. Was this the part where he was going to send Trey to his room and then beat the air out of my lungs? My fists clenched up in fright, ready to defend myself however futilely. This was our life. This was what I knew when it came to being with J. It was rather depressing to admit to myself that this was what I was returning to.

"We're going to go lay down," he informed me. "Just us. You can stay out here and do whatever. I'll get up when I get up." With that, he scooped Trey once more and disappeared to the bedroom that we once shared.

I stood in the middle of the living room for a moment afraid to exhale. He hadn't threatened me or laid a hand on me. Though his tone was icy, he hadn't done anything volatile or aggressive. I was shocked but I didn't want to fool myself into believing that my husband had turned over a new leaf. If anything, it was just a matter of time before he began to show his true colors and prove himself to be the abusive man that he was. Still, I was grateful that there was silence and peace, however temporary it was. I didn't protest his decision to share the bedroom with Trey. I didn't mind at all the distance he was putting between us. It was far better than him beating me or coming on to me and forcing me to have sex. Once I accepted that he was not going to pounce of me right then, I curled up on the sofa and decided to take a nap myself. After the long uncomfortable ride back to Texas and the hours that Trey and I had spent out on the back lawn, my body needed to rest as comfortably as possible. It took a while for sleep to come to me yet even when it did I tossed and turned and was barely able to relax for fear that J would beat me out of my sleep. This was the life I'd returned to. It just wasn't fair.

***

Later, when we'd all awaken J told me that he was taking off from work and spending the day with Trey. I figured it was a good gesture towards trying to rebuild their father-son relationship. As long as he didn't try to run off and skip town with Trey, I didn't mind their one-on-one time. In their absence, I kept myself occupied by straightening up the house. As I moved from room to room, re-acclimating myself with the space that I called home, I couldn't help but notice things. Firstly, there was a cordless phone plugged up and resting on its cradle. I lifted the receiver and pressed the TALK button just to see if there was an actual working phone line. The sound of the dial tone amazed me. Quickly, I turned the phone off and returned it to the cradle while wondering what had made J have a change of heart about having a phone in the house. Had he done it for me upon anticipating our return home? Had he done it for himself although he relied on his cell phone?

Moving back into the living room, my mind ran from one thought to another as I vacuumed. My thoughts all came to a halt the moment I saw a pair of black pumps resting at the far end of the sofa. I shut off the vacuum cleaner and bent down to pick up the left shoe. I didn't need to inspect them to know that they weren't mine. But, I took a look at the underside to check the size anyway. They were a size eight and I wore a size ten. It was clear to me that J had been entertaining someone regularly enough for the woman to have left her shoes behind. I simply replaced the shoe on the ground and set the pair up against the wall neatly. Even though I knew that J was a bad husband, I still felt a tinge of betrayal at the tangible evidence of his infidelity. Before one tear could fall from my swollen eyes I reminded myself that this was the same man that had knocked me around without any remorse. Did I really expect him to be faithful to me especially during the time when he was threatening to kill me if I didn't return our son to him?

So I carried on with my cleaning and tried to put the shoes of the phantom woman out of my mind. While cleaning the bathroom, I opened the cabinet underneath the sink to retrieve the cleaning supplies and was surprised to find random framed photos of us as a family stuffed away behind a few bottles. I pulled them out to look at them, remembering a time when I thought we were happy and realizing that he'd hidden our memories so that whoever the phantom woman was wouldn't see them. It dawned on me that he must have been lying to her, trying to make it appear as though he was a single man with no children. I shook my head. He didn't want the world to know that we existed but he was ready to commit murder if he couldn't have us there within his reach. Sighing deeply, I returned the photos to their hiding places and was resigned to never mention it to him. I didn't want to do or say anything that was going to cause him to be upset with me and thus lash out.

As I cleaned and cleaned, my thoughts continued to run rampant. Was that it? Had I figured out the key to staying alive and keeping J in good spirits? Maybe if I just shut up and never did or said anything to press his buttons then we could possibly get back to a tenth of the way things used to be. If I put all of my energy into making our house a loving home and not doing anything to anger him, then maybe J would become a better husband. It made perfect sense in my brain as I went from room to room trying to make everything perfect. For days I did just that, worked on keeping my mouth shut and doing nothing but making sure that the house was clean and that J had whatever it was that he needed. I tried to be the docile, sweet, attentive wife that I thought he wanted me to be. I even called him in the middle of the day just to tell him that I hoped he was having a good day. When I didn't receive an answer, I didn't let it deter me from the new mindset that I had. If I had to be in this marriage with this monster of a man, perhaps I could redirect his hostility, temper, and emotions by being a better me. By this point, I'd internalized everything that had happened in our marriage deciding that I was the key to it all and with that being so I was more determined than ever to make things work.

***

Trey was coloring at the kitchen table and I'd just decided upon what I was going to make for dinner. To my surprise, I heard the garage door open and close and then in walked J with a bouquet of two dozen pink roses and a huge smile on his face. I was speechless as he entered the kitchen. Staring at him, I saw hints of the man that I'd first fallen in love with but I couldn't help but wonder if I was dreaming in the moment.

"Hey son," he greeted Trey. "Had a good day?"

Even Trey was astonished by his father's upbeat mood. He nodded and smiled awkwardly, not knowing what to expect.

J waltzed over to me and planted a kiss right against my lips. I didn't have an opportunity to react before he placed the flowers in my hands and lowered himself to his knees while looking up at me with sincere eyes.

"Melissa," he said softly. "I know things haven't been perfect but I'd really like for you to be my wife again."

The proposal took my breath away. Again, I wondered if I was dreaming. I'd longed for him to come to his senses and realize what a good thing he had. To see him coming to me with humility and genuineness brought tears to my eyes. I felt that all of my extra efforts to be a good wife had paid off and now he was willing to be the good husband that I needed him to be.

"I wanna make things right," he told me. "Can we do that? Can you let me try to do that?"

I'd be lying if I said that I wouldn't have given anything to have my family back intact and have a healthy relationship with the man who had once made me feel like silk. I nodded my consent, unable to say a word for my voice was stuck in my throat as I choked by the tears of relief that had come over me.

J smiled as he jumped back to a standing position. “Okay, let’s get you all changed and dolled up. I’m taking you guys out to dinner.”

So much for me having to cook. I liked this side of J. He was really beginning to act like a family man and I appreciated it. I got myself and Trey changed and as promised, J took us out to a steak house and for the first time in a long time we actually enjoyed one another’s company. It was as if we’d traveled back in time and none of the somberness or heartache associated with our relationship existed. By the time we returned home and I’d put Trey to bed, my heart was fluttering. I didn’t know what to expect or how I was supposed to feel. It all seemed so surreal as I stood in our bathroom preparing myself to share a bed with my husband willingly after so long. I chose to put on a leopard print camisole and capri pants night set. It was sexy and feminine without being overly provocative. I didn’t want to send J the message that I was necessarily ready to be intimate with him then and there, but I wanted him to remember how beautiful he once viewed me as.

Slowly, I exited the bathroom to find J already laying on his side of the bed in just his lounging pants. His eyes never left me as I eased onto the bed beside him. I sat awkwardly upright not knowing what I should do next. I didn't feel comfortable leaning over to lay on him and I didn't want to lay back as if inviting him to take over my body. Silence lingered between us as we both sorted out our own thoughts.

"Just say it," he finally said.

I looked over at him confusedly. "Just say what?"

"Whatever's on your mind. You haven't really said much."

"Well, I'm not sure what to say…I mean, I'm not sure what any of this means," I replied meekly. "Today was wonderful…it's been a long time since we've been out or you've been…you know…nice."

"I know, I know. And I promise you that I'll never be unkind again."

I stared at him hard. "Truthfully, when we first came home I thought you were going to kill me. I was afraid to so much as go to sleep."

"I'm sorry for that."

I just looked at him for a moment before going on. "Do you have any idea how that feels? Being afraid to go to sleep in your own home? Afraid that your own spouse will kill you?"

J shook his head. "I know that you must have been really scared with the way I was carrying on…and you have every right to be. But, it won't happen again, Melissa. You have my word. I was wrong, baby, and it won't ever happen again."

A tear trickled down my cheek. I wanted to believe him; my spirit needed to believe that he meant everything he was saying, but I wasn't so sure. "Do you remember some of the things you said to me, J? I really…I really felt like you didn't love me anymore…and there were times when I wanted to die. I tried…" The words could barely come out as my emotions took over. "I tried to kill myself once."

His eyes widened and then restored to their normal height as he reached over and grabbed my left hand. "I'm so sorry," he said, kissing the back of my hand over and over again. "I'm so, so sorry. I didn't know. I had no idea. I take full responsibility for everything that's happened and I promise you that I've changed. You never have to worry about any of that again, I swear it. Just please…trust me and don't leave me, Melissa. Let me show you that things can be good between us again.

"And the women?" I asked, referring to the cheating that he'd been doing.

"Thing of the past," he assured me. "All I care about is you and Trey. That's all I want."

It all sounded good. He was saying all of the things that I needed to hear and it sounded perfect, but something just didn't feel right deep within my spirit. I couldn't put my finger on it, but something was nagging at me making me feel as if this was just another great farce that my husband was putting on. I tried to ignore my intuition. I tried as hard as I could to block out that little voice in my head that was telling me that something wasn't right.

J placed his arms around me in a tight embrace. "I've got you. All of that stuff is behind us now. You can trust me, Melissa. I love you."

I love you. Those were three very powerful words that I hadn't heard my husband say in a long time. Who doesn't want to be loved especially after being so mistreated and broken for such a long time? It was a welcomed change to hear my husband speak to me with affection and to feel him touching me in a way that wouldn't leave my skin bruised the next day. I closed my eyes and allowed him to hold me a few moments longer. In the darkness of my covered pupils I saw a clear image of the shoes that had been resting near the sofa; the heels that didn't belong to me. It was a conscience reminder of what J was capable of and what I should be leery of. Still, I wanted to give my husband the benefit of the doubt I wanted us to work out.

~ Chapter 9~
Revelations

"Truth is like the sun. You can shut it out for a time, but it ain't goin' away." –Elvis Presley

I woke up to the sound of the smell of sizzling bacon and the sweet batter of pancakes. I wasn't sure if my senses were playing tricks on me, but my mouth was watering from the moment the sunlight assaulted my eyes. I rose from the bed, cleaned myself up and got dressed, and then made the trek down to the kitchen where Trey was sitting at the table stuffing his face with oddly shaped pancakes. J was standing at the stove, fully dressed and covered by an apron, flipping what appeared to be the last batch of pancakes.

"What's all this?" I asked, peering and smiling at him. I hadn't seen him get down in the kitchen in quite some time. The new behaviors he was displaying were really starting to make me feel more secure in his declaration of wanting to start over.

"Thought I'd whip up a little breakfast for you for a change," he told me, stepping back to place a kiss upon my cheek. He threw three pancakes onto a plate filled with crisp bacon and handed it to me. "Enjoy, love."

"You're not eating with me?" I asked, kind of wanting to enjoy his company as I dined.

"Gotta go to work." He walked over to Trey and began wiping him down with a damp towel. "Come on, little man. Gotta get you cleaned up."

I sat my plate on the table and took my seat. "It's okay, I can clean him up when I'm done."

"Naw, he's going to work with me."

I was surprised. "Seriously? Is it bringing your child to work day?" I didn't mean it sarcastically but the second the words left my lips I wanted to snatch them back. The last thing I needed was for J to feel as if I was being an ass. We were getting along so well and I didn't want my tone or word choice to do anything to set us back.

"No. I'm only working half a day so it's cool. Besides, the job knows how sick you've been and they know that I need to be around to make sure you're good now that you're back home."

I had no idea that he'd so much as mentioned me to his superiors yet along worked it out with them to be able to tend to me although I was fine at the current moment. I didn't question his plan any further. If he wanted to take his son to work with him and this employer was okay with a one-year-old hanging around, then who was I to question it? I simply, tore into my breakfast and felt blessed that I had a husband who saw fit to make sure that I was straight before running off to make his living.

"I'll be back around noon-ish," he informed me, taking our son by his hand and heading towards the door. "Take it easy. Go back to bed or something and I'll see you soon."

That sounded like a great plan to me. "Have a good morning," I said to my menfolk as they exited. After finishing my breakfast and cleaning up the kitchen, I took J up on his advice and crawled right back into bed. It felt good to be able to just lay about for a while and do nothing. It felt even better to not be stressing over whether or not I'd get slapped or punched later in the day. I felt that maybe life really was settling down for us and it felt good just to revel in that moment of peace.

True to his word, J returned around noon with a slew of groceries in tow. I marveled over the things that he pulled out of the plastic bags as I helped him to put them away. Gone was that ridiculous $50 grocery budget he'd stuck me with previously. Although he hadn't asked me what I wanted from the store, I was grateful that he'd had the mindset to provide Trey and I with more than just a few items that would only leave us starving by the week's end. After the groceries were away, he shocked me again by volunteering to go with me to wash all of me and Trey's clothes. It was refreshing to be splitting household responsibilities with my husband verses being treated as a lowly servant to him.

With the chores all done, I decided to cook him a great dinner since he'd been so wonderful to us. I was more than happy to treat my man like the king he was behaving as. I steamed some broccoli, made mashed potatoes from scratch, and was smothering some chicken breasts while a fresh pan of cornbread muffins baked in the oven. As I was chopping up veggies to toss over in the skillet with the smothered chicken, I felt hands quickly clasp on top of my shoulders and his voice booming in my ear.

"Boo!"

I nearly jumped out of my skin in response to the shock. I dropped the knife onto the floor after cutting my finger. My scream resonated throughout the house causing Trey to trod to the threshold of the kitchen door. My eyes locked with J's as he laughed heartily. "Don't do that!" I hollered at him. "It isn't funny." I wanted to cry, but instead I turned around and shoved my finger under a stream of cold water from the faucet.

"Why are you scared?" he asked me

Because I'm used to you coming out of nowhere and knocking the shit out of me, I wanted to say. But, I caught myself before I could respond. It was a stupid question and it was a stupid thing for him to do, but I didn't want to argue or fight and I didn't want to say anything that was going to set him off and place us in a bad position when he was working so hard to prove that he was still the man I'd fallen in love with.

J folded his arms and leaned up against the counter beside me as I picked up the knife and washed it off. "Can I ask you a question?"

"Mmmhmm."

"Why'd you leave? Why'd you take Trey and just jet outta know where like that?"

The question came out of nowhere and I saw it as nothing but a downhill slope in the progression of our relationship. Maybe if he had asked during our open discussion in bed or even when I first got home, but at that point when we were in the throes of repairing us it just didn't feel like a topic we were safe covering at that moment. I remained silent as I emptied the peppers and onions into the skillet over the meat.

"I just wanna know," he said. I could feel his eyes boring holes into the side of my skull. "Why?"

"Why are we talking about this?" I retorted. "It's over and done now, J. I'm back. We're moving on…"

Lighting fast, J took off and snatched Trey up from where he'd begun playing in the doorway. I turned to watch him run off with our son and raced to the hallway to see what was going on.

"What are you doing? Where are you taking him?" I called out. My brain was racing. I wasn't sure where J's mindset was or what he was up to, but didn't know how to proceed. As I tried to figure out my next move I watched him return and felt a heightened sense of anxiety as he grabbed my arm and pulled me back into the kitchen.

"We need to talk," he said through gritted teeth as he stood close to me, staring into my eyes.

"Why'd you take him to his room? What is it that we need to discuss that's got you so upset?" I had no clue how we'd gotten to this place we were in but I was afraid of the outcome.

"I don't want to be with you anymore," he said with little to no feelings.

I was baffled and thought that maybe I wasn't hearing him correctly. "What?" I whispered. Surely this wasn't the man that I'd been getting reacquainted with.

"I don't want to be with you," he repeated in a heated tone moving forward causing me to back up towards the stove. "In fact, I hate you!" he seethed.

"What is wrong with you?" I asked, afraid of the monster he was returning to right before my eyes.

"You think that you could just take my kid and leave me and everything be all good? Who do you think you are? I wanted to kill you! I wanted to squeeze the life out of your scrawny little neck."

I was pressed against the stove, scared for my life. I knew that it was all too good to be true and here he was proving himself to be the demon that he'd been to me all this time. "What's wrong with you?" I asked him again. "Was this your plan? Is that why you called me to come back here? So you could pay me back for what you think I've done to you?"

He laughed evilly and turned his back to me as he moved over to the refrigerator. My eyes darted over to the doorway and I tried to guesstimate whether or not I could make a run for it. I didn't want to stand there and wait to see what kind of hell he was going to condemn me to. All of my wishes for a better life were shot to hell now. It was time for me to go into survival mode. Before I could make a move, J turned around quickly and the next thing I knew a sharp pain emanated from my forehead and immediately blood began to drip from my eyebrow. I saw the bottle opener that he'd thrown at me like a dart as it now rested on the floor. My hand flew up to wipe away at the liquid that was spilling from my face. My scream was delayed but once it came out it was earsplitting. It caused my son to come running from his room to see what was happening. By the time he reached the doorway, J had already pounced on me and had me cowering up against the oven on the floor, slipping around on the linoleum in the tracks of my blood.

"Nooo!" Trey screamed out. "No, Daddy! No." His little fist pounded on his father's back to no avail. As J's arm revved back to issue yet another blow to my body, Trey tried to grab it. But, J yanked away from him so forcefully that it caused our son to fall back onto his behind.

I heard him cry out and instantly I knew that this entire ordeal was my fault. I should have never brought my son back into this madness and I should have never believed that J had changed his ways. I watched as J removed himself from me and headed over to snatch up Trey.

"No!" I screamed, trying to get up and run after him as he exited the kitchen. I slipped twice because of the red liquid underneath my feet, but I forced myself to move forward. I dashed through the hall and made it up to Trey's room just as J slammed the door shut.

"Mommy! Mommy!" I could hear my son crying and screaming for me on the other side. His tiny fist pounded against the door and then it sounded as if he'd begun to kick as he continuously tried to turn the knob to no avail.

"What are you doing?" I asked J manically. "What are you doing? Why are you locking him in there?" I tried to brush past him and reach for the knob, but J grabbed me by my aching waist. "Let him out!" I screamed. "Let my son out of there!"

J carried me to our room, slamming the door shut behind him. A flashback to a previous incident we'd had occurred to me and I knew without a shadow of a doubt that this was it. He was going to make good on his threats and finally kill me. I shuddered to think of what he was going to do to our son after the deed was done. He dropped me to the floor causing me to hit my head on the railing of the bed but I didn't give in to the searing pain that jolted through my skull. I looked up at him as he towered over me with that menacing look on his face that I'd become all too familiar with. In this moment, I hated him and if I had any strength at all my only wish was to murder him before he had the chance to end my life.

"Why are you doing this?" I asked him as my chest rose and fell with fear and anguish. "Why are you taking us through all of this? If you want me to leave, then fine. I'll go. But what kind of man are you, what kind of father are you, to be constantly filling your son's life with this kind of pain?"

He stared at me for a moment as if he was really contemplating the insult I'd just issued him. I watched intently as he backed away from me and crossed the room with his back to me and his head down. I didn't know what he was going through or what he was about to do next but I knew that I couldn't just sit there and wait on it. Without thinking it through any further, I rose from the floor and bolted out of the bedroom door. I wasn't leaving the house though I'm sure that's what he thought my intentions were. I wasn't about to leave that crazy man alone with my son while I was still able to breathe. I was intent upon fighting for my life and since he was bigger and stronger than me I knew that I needed something far more deadly than my bare hands if I wanted to have a fighting chance. I could hear my baby hollering and going hoarse from the prison his father had placed him in. J pursued me as I knew he would, I just prayed that I had time to pick it up before he caught up to me. I bee lined for the kitchen and headed over to the counter where I'd left the knife and cutting board. I felt a tinge of power as my arm outstretched to reach for the knife but the universe was not working in my favor as I felt myself slip on the wet linoleum floor. My heart sunk into my stomach as I heard and felt J come up behind me. I knew then - it was over.

I looked up at J in fright. My mouth opened but no words came out. I held my hands up as if to surrender and I shook my head briskly as if begging him not to hurt me anymore. J ignored my pitiful attempts to ward him off. He reached over and grabbed the simmering pan of smothered chicken and before I could back up or crawl away to safety, he threw the hot contents of the pan onto my face.

"Ahhhhh!" I screamed mercifully as I frantically peeled chicken and vegetables from my face. Sauce from the food had splattered into my eyes and I could barely see.

J capitalized on my vulnerability and immediately begun to punch me repeatedly in my rib cage and stomach. After a while my screams subsided as the pain consumed me and shortly after that my body stopped moving. J's blows didn't cease until after he'd grown tired of punching my badly bruised and contorted body. Only then did he back away from me and race out of the room. I could hear him moving about around the house. The sounds of Trey's cries grew louder and I could tell that J had freed him. Instantly I feared that my husband was taking my son and leaving me to die right there on the kitchen floor. I couldn't move. All I could do was lay there with tears running into my ears, blood and gravy blinding my eyes, pain claiming my body. Soon, I heard a door open and close followed by the sound of J's truck peeling out of the garage.

Little spurts of heavy breathing filled the room just as little hands touched my face. "Mommy?" Trey called my name. "Get up, Ma-Ma. Get up." I could tell by the sound of his voice that he was terrified.

Food and blood were everywhere. The kitchen looked as if there'd been an all-out war when in fact there had only been one single jumping as my husband had pounced on me and did his best to take me out. I was beginning to pass in and out but I tried my best to concentrate on the sound of Trey's breathing and his pleas for me to get up.

"Get…the…phone," I managed to whisper to him. "Get Ma-Ma the phone."

"Phone?" Trey repeated before dashing out of the kitchen to retrieve the cordless phone that I was ever so grateful to J for installing in our house. Seconds later he returned and placed the phone in my hand.

I struggled to dial the numbers, 911, and even after the emergency operator came on the line, it took everything in me to give her the address and briefly describe my situation. I knew that time was of the essence and that if I didn't get help soon my son would be motherless. It took about five minutes for the ambulance to arrive at which time I was grateful to J once more for moving so fast that he'd neglected to lock the door. The paramedics came right in and Trey was such a big boy to lead them over to me. Once I knew that I was in good hands and that my son would be okay for now, I allowed myself to slip away for a moment. Holding on was so hard and the pain was so great that I just needed a moment to hide in the darkness.

***

"Where am I?" I sat up and looked around at all of the machines and the unfamiliar face that was perched upon the bed to my left. "Where am I?" I asked again, this time in a more forceful tone.

"You're in ICU at the hospital," the man in the white coat answered me. "You suffered some internal bleeding and a broken rib. You were in critical condition when you came in and we still have some concerns regarding that bleeding." The doctor leaned in closer. "This isn't good, Melissa. You could have very well died before they got you to the hospital and even in the operating room."

The intensity of his voice made me lean back against the pillows of my hospital bed. But, it was the presence of the police officer that entered the room right after that made my heart rate quicken. The reality of it all was sinking in. J had almost succeeded in killing me this time. Per this doctor's assessment, I was lucky to be alive. Trey was lucky to still have a mother.

"My son," I stated in a panic. "Where's my son?"

"He's safe," the doctor stated. "We have him in the family room being watched by a nurse for now. We needed to get an emergency contact for you so that we can hand him over to someone that can be responsible for him. The next option was to call in social services."

"Social Services," I repeated, growing even more afraid of the position I was finding myself in.

"Who did this to you?" the doctor asked.

I remained silent.

"You're young," the doctor stated. "And beautiful and I'm sure full of potential. But you're hanging on here by a thread, Melissa. What happened to you wasn't something you deserved and whoever did it…you owe them nothing. But that kid of yours down the hall, he deserves for you to be at your strongest right now and alleviate ever having to find either of you in this position again."

"Ma'am," the officer spoke up. "I'm Officer Warren. From the looks of things, you've been the victim of a domestic dispute and it's up to you whether or not you press charges. But I can tell you that majority of the cases I get called on where the woman refuses to name her abuser and declines making a report…those women typically don't make it out alive the next time."

I felt my face grow wet and my mouth grow parched as I struggled to speak up. "I want…I want to file a report," I said. "My husband's been beating me…he did this. My husband tried to kill me."

I was proud of myself for finally documenting J's abuse. After filing the report, the police then encouraged me to get a restraining order which stated that J wasn't allowed within a hundred yards of me or Trey. He wasn't even allowed to so much as call us. After the doctor signed off on my discharge, I was referred to a private counselor by the hospital psychologist that I'd been mandated to see before being discharged. I had nothing: no money, no car, and no way to get to a train station in order to get home. The hospital staff had been kind enough to let Trey stay with me as I was afraid to get any of my family members involved in the mess that I was trying so hard to get myself out of. Upon returning home it was evident that J hadn't returned. I locked the doors and even though Trey and I went to bed that night, I barely slept. I kept a knife by my side so that I'd be prepared should he decide to sneak up on me.

I was trying to plot out my next move. I knew that I couldn't afford to continue staying in the house. Without J's financial assistance I knew that Trey and I would be sitting in the dark cold with no food, electricity, or any other means of surviving. I knew that I was going to have to start over from scratch and that meant that I would have to be completely transparent with my family and solicit their help. As I sat in the living room the next day after returning home, my heart began to pound the moment I heard his truck pull into the garage. Immediately, I grabbed the knife that I kept beside me and told Trey to go to his room and play quietly. By now I was certain that the police had found him and served him with the restraining order, but J being him, he was defiant and there he was showing up at our home as if nothing had happened.

I stood there staring at him as he entered through the kitchen and crossed over into the living room. In my mind I dared him to make a move. I was no longer afraid of him and I was ready to slice his neck from one end to the other if he even looked as if he wanted to lay a hand on me. Self-defense was all I had to say in defending my actions. He wasn't supposed to be there and I damn sure wasn't about to let him use my body for a punching bag any more.

"You have to pack your stuff," he said.

My eyebrow rose. He'd practically beat me unconscious and now he was coming back to put me out? He should have just done that in the first place and I would have gladly vacated the premises without putting up a fight. "You should pack your stuff," I told him. "And once we're gone you can have your house back."

"We all have to pack," he replied. "I got orders to move out to Columbus, Georgia effective next week."

A light bulb went off in my mind. Here was my out. If I could go back to Georgia with him and he just drop Trey and I off, then we could both wash our hands of one another and move on. But, I didn't know if he could be trusted.

"We're not going with you," I told him.

He shrugged. "I guess not since you're trying to have me arrested. I'm still gonna pack my things if you don't mind."

I nodded and watched as he headed towards our bedroom. "If you promise not to touch me, not to try anything stupid then we'll ride out with you. But we won't live with you. We're not going to Columbus with you. I'm done with this, J. I'm going back to my family, Trey and I. If you so much as lay a finger on me and I live to tell about it, I swear I'll either kill you myself or I'll make sure that they throw your ass under the jail."

J looked at me but didn't say a word. I could tell that this aggressive side of me caught him off-guard. He didn't want to go to jail. My actions now were showing him that I was serious about not allowing him to run over me. For the longest he'd assumed that he could just do whatever he wanted to me and I would just take it and take it and take it. Those days were over. I was determined not to allow him to get the best of me or push me into an early grave. Trey needed me and I wasn't about to let his sorry excuse for a father hamper me from being the best possible mother that I could to his son.

And it was so; we spent the next week in the same house packing our things up and preparing to vacate the home. I continued to carry my knife with me all over the house just in case he took leave of his senses and decided to do something stupid. He never did. The thought of ending up in jail surely motivated him to keep his hands to himself. We barely spoke; there was no need to. There was nothing else between us that needed to be worked out or discussed. When the time came, Trey and I traveled with J back to Georgia. I'd already arranged my stay with Charlene and she was more than pleased to have Trey and I back at her home. By that point I'd broken down and told my siblings the truth about my marriage and my husband. I needed them to know what all I'd been through and what I was going through so that they would be prepared to act accordingly should J decided to renege on our agreement and kidnap or kill me. He knew that my entire family was waiting for me to safely make it to Atlanta and that if I didn't do so by a certain time, the police would be searching for him.

It felt good to be reclaiming my life. I was hesitant about burdening my sister and her family, but she assured me that they wanted nothing more than to help me get back on my feet. I was apprehensive about starting over and finding a job so that I could support myself and my child, but Charlene and my other family members were right there helping me along as I filled out application after application while trying to remain encouraged. I knew that the road to self-sufficiency would be long and hard but this time around I wasn't backtracking. I knew what needed to be done and I knew that I wasn't going to settle for returning to the life of fear and heartache that had constituted my marriage. I was delivered from that hell of a situation and it was time for me to start letting my light shine once again.

~ Chapter 10~
Divorce

"Divorce isn't such a tragedy. A tragedy's staying in an unhappy marriage, teaching your children the wrong things about love. Nobody ever died of divorce." –Jennifer Weiner, *Fly Away Home*

With me being as sick as I was, I had to right away find a primary care provider and schedule a follow up appointment immediately upon arriving at my sister's house in Atlanta. I received a second chance at a full and happy life so I was going to make the best out of it. First things first, I needed to take care of my health. After calling Dr. Xu's office I was given a referral to a reputable doctor in Atlanta. I was able to schedule an appointment the same week of my arrival. When I got to the doctor's office I gave the receptionist all of the information that I had--my insurance card and my sister's address. Things seemed to go smoothly. My new doctor, Dr. Weber was very kind and thorough. We went through a routine visit and I was sent on my way.

Before I could exit the office suite, I was stopped by the office's billing manager. "Mrs. January," she called out. "I need to speak to you for a second."

I turned and gave her a perplexed look. "Yes?"

"Your insurance info is no longer available for you," she said in a whispered tone.

My eyebrow rose. "What do you mean?" I asked in a not so whispered tone.

She looked at the other patients sitting in the waiting room and motioned towards the door leading to the suite's offices and examine rooms. "Can you come with me? We can talk about this in my office."

I followed her to the back and into her corner office where she closed the door and encouraged me to take a seat. Seated in front of her computer, I guess looking at my digital file, she shook her head. "Yeah, we're unable to find you in the Tricare system, dear."

"There must be a mistake," I said. "Let me call them."

"I've tried that and they confirmed that you were not a subscriber but by all means if you think you can get it cleared up—"

"May I use your phone?"

"Of course." She turned her desk phone in my direction.

I dialed the customer service number on the back of my insurance card and gave the representative my name and birthdate. I explained that my husband was the sponsor and gave his information as well.

"Hmmm, Ma'am, it looks like you're no longer covered," the rep stated.

"But I've always been covered," I said, dumbfounded.

"Yes, I see were you were covered but given your current circumstances you're no longer covered under Jason January's policy."

"That's ridiculous! Can you explain why that is, please?"

"Sure, once we got the notification from your husband concerning your divorce by law we had to remove you from his policy."

I stared at the billing manager in disbelief. Had I heard this guy correctly? "Umm…" I could barely find the words to respond. "You said he send you some kind of notification? So you have actual proof on file?"

"Yes, Ma'am. Mr. January provided a copy of your divorce decree about two months ago."

I hung up. I could not believe that J would go that far. No one wanted us to be divorced more than I did, but there was a way to handle things. The way he'd gone about it was completely childish. I was appalled. The whole time he'd been bothering me about working it out and trying to sleep with me he'd already gone behind my back and divorced me. Now I was going to be stuck with a huge medical bill.

"Is everything okay?" the billing coordinator asked me.

"I-I-I just need…umm…I just need a moment," I told her.

She hesitated for a moment before scrolling down the page on her screen. "So…if you'd like we can set up monthly payments for the services rendered. We can work with you and what's comfortable for you right now," she said sympathetically.

Tears built up in my eyes. "Nothing's comfortable for me. I don't even have a job. With my condition I'm not even able to work."

"How about this," she said. "We can give you a couple of options to review once you're…uh, stable and focused. Then you can call us back in a day or two and we'll work something out. Okay?"

I nodded.

She printed a paper with the payment options and I left the office as quickly as I could. I was livid and needed to figure out immediately what was up with this alleged divorce decree. I just couldn't phantom the idea that J had really gone through the whole divorce process legally without my knowledge. The first thing I did was call the courthouse. Although we were not married in Georgia the clerk was able to cross reference records for citizens and saw that we were still listed as married. She then told me that sometimes it took time for a divorce to process in the system after being granted.

I was dismayed. "So, how can I find out if I'm really divorced then?" I asked feeling frustrated.

"You should have gotten a divorce decree."

I wanted to bang my sister's phone against the wall. "My insurance company told me that my husband gave them a copy of the divorce decree that he received. I didn't even know that he was divorcing me. Now I just need proof of it."

"Well, the plaintiff doesn't have to notify the defendant personally about a divorce claim."

"Excuse me?" She was making no sense to me and I was losing my patience.

"You can place an ad in the newspaper and if the other party doesn't respond the judge will just go ahead and grant the divorce to the person who is filing for it."

"Wow," I whispered. "So…if a divorce decree exists for real how do I get it?"

"Where you divorced here in Georgia?"

"No…I just moved here so--"

"You have to call the courthouse where the divorce was granted then, honey. They should have the papers on file there."

"Thank you." I hung up the phone and shook my head.

This was getting wilder and wilder by the second. I knew that J was a low-down, dirty dog but this was a new low for him. I looked up the number to the courthouse in Killeen and placed a call to them. After telling them who I was and what I needed, I was placed on hold. Those few seconds had my mind whirling in awe of how my husband had basically discarded me like I was nothing.

"Ma'am?" the clerk said, returning to the line.

"Yes," I answered.

"Okay, yes. We have your divorce decree on file."

I took a deep breath. “How did this happen?” I whispered, leaning back against the pillows on the couch.

“It appears that his attorney placed an ad in the paper which you had seven days to respond.”

“How was I supposed to respond? I never got a paper! I was sick…in the hospital.”

A pause. “Okay. I’m sorry to hear that,” she responded.

I pursed my lips to keep from spewing venom into her ear. It wasn’t her fault that my husband was an ass. “Okay, can I please receive a copy of my divorce papers?”

“Sure, provide me with your mailing address and we’ll send them to you in about fourteen business days.”

I rattled off my sister’s address for her and hung up the phone after issuing a curt thank you. Holding the phone, I thought about the situation. It was totally messed up how he handled it but the end result was undeniably beautiful--I was free.

A little over a week later I received a certified letter in the mail from the Superior Court of Texas. I settled Trey in front of the television to watch an episode of *Super Why* while eating his afternoon snack. I sat on the sofa and opened the envelope with trembling hands. My eyes couldn't believe what I was reading. Per my divorce decree, J and I had been divorced nearly a year ago and didn't share any children. It even stated that we'd separated in 2006 but I was still living in Germany at that time. The lies just seemed to fill up the page. I lowered the papers and glanced over at a squealing Trey. He was such a beautiful child. My chest was hurting from the knowledge of J denying his son, the very same son that he begged me to have.

It was all too much. I stuffed the papers back into the envelope. I didn't want to read anymore. It was very clear that J had no intentions of ever being in our son's life and that was for the best. We didn't need him. Looking at Trey I knew that I had to hustle to get our life in order. I was ready to jump on any opportunity that came my way. It was time to create a stable life for my son and I. I owed Trey a life full of joy and happiness. He'd suffered due to my lapse of judgment for far too long. That period of our life was over. We were embarking upon the beginning of better times.

***

Just when I was finally happy and piecing my life together, I was reminded of the past. I'd gotten over J and his foolishness, forgiven myself for the role I played, and successfully moved on. I thought it was over until the day I received a message on Facebook:

> **D.M:** Hey I know you don't know me but the only way I found you is cause your name's tattooed on his arm… and I wanted to just see if he was lying to me. I'm sorry for coming to you on Facebook… but it was the only way I knew how to get ahold of you.
>
> **ME:** And who has my name on his arm? I was genuinely confused by the message and its sender.
>
> **D.M:** J
>
> **ME:** That's funny.
>
> **D.M:** I have not seen him in a while since he is in Iraq… I just wanted to see if you guys

were really divorced. I know it is crazy me in boxing you but for some reason he has been trying to talk to me and I just found out he had a baby in August.

ME: Yes, we're divorced. We do have a child together.

D.M: Yeah, Trey, right? I was pregnant by him while he was stationed in Texas. And one day I checked his cell phone and some girl was calling him and they were engaged too. Which was funny cause we both had rings. Guess he got money like that. He has been emailing me asking if we are going to be together when he comes back. His homeboy told me that before he got to Texas he was in Colorado and had a little girl there. So I guess he got about 5 kids now.

As I read the words my hand flew to my mouth. Whoever this was she was telling it all. Apparently, J had been living quite a double life and I wasn't the only woman whose heart he'd broken. The thought of him sleeping with multiple women yet still trying to sleep with me sickened me. I mean, I assumed that he was cheating since he never stayed home, but having confirmation of it was almost as devastating as the myriad of lies he'd included in our divorce papers. I wondered if he'd put his hands on other women as well.

> **ME:** Well when he was in Texas we were still married. I was in a coma while he was out there getting engaged and having babies. Wow!

> **D.M:** Oh my God are you serious? He was what? He was still with you??? That is crazy I had a miscarriage November 2007. He would drop of Trey at my house all the time and just leave. I have tons of pictures of him when he had long hair. You really have the most adorable little boy.

The thought of J leaving my son with some random woman boiled my blood. I didn't even know where he was, but I wanted to find him and strangle him.

> **ME:** Thank you.

D.M: I did not even know you were in Texas with him. He told me he had divorced you and took Trey. He is such a weirdo…what a liar!

Since moving to Atlanta and receiving the divorce papers I'd developed a certain level of peace that was threatening to be disrupted by the continuation of this conversation. I couldn't allow myself to slip back into a place where I cared so much about what J did or didn't do.

ME: I don't have any more comments about this dude. It's clear that he is playing every woman he meets. I am just glad I'm not a part of this anymore.

D.M: I am sorry he did that to you.

ME: Don't be sorry, you didn't know.

D.M: After I had my miscarriage he hit me and I left him. I just thought it was funny how after a year later almost he is still trying to talk to me. I just been emailing him. I have no intention of ever getting back with him. He has too many kids. LOL! And definitely has a lot of problems. That' s why he hurried up and left Texas. He was going to get in trouble because of the girl that was pregnant in Colorado. She called his 1st Sgt.

ME: Interesting.

I wanted to tell her to shut up, to not tell me anything else. In my mind I'd already decided that I didn't care and didn't want to know anymore.

D.M: He told me he's trying to go to Columbus, GA. He been asking me to move there with him.

I stopped responding. I couldn't take anymore. I blocked the sender so that she couldn't give me any more information of which to make me revert back to the Melissa that crumbled at the thought of being so mistreated by the man I'd given my all too. No matter how far I'd come from that broken woman he'd turned me into, the truth was that it still hurt. I learned that it would continue to hurt for a long time, but even in that moment I knew that there was hope. I knew that I would eventually find someone to love and honor me the way I deserved. I knew that I would be able to give my son the world because I loved him more than anything. I knew that overtime the emotional ties that I had with J would vanish as time heals all wounds. Most importantly, I knew that I could never again let another person hold so much power over my life.

For years I remained silent about it all. Even my family didn't know the complete truth about all the horrible things I endured at the hands of my husband. But, I won't hide in the shadows and keep my secrets to myself anymore. I won't pretend that nothing happened and just shove it aside. I am a survivor. And I am NOT afraid to talk about it anymore. I am NOT alone anymore. I am at peace. And if I, little ole me, can survive the things that I did and be okay then anyone can survive! All you have to do is want more for yourself. The rest will fall into place. You just have to work towards making it happen.

Given all that I been through and all that I've learned, I realize that it is my responsibility to help other people take that first little step towards healing because that's all it takes--just one step. God, the Universe, or whatever you call it, will do the rest. Everything happens for a reason. If you're reading this right now, there's a purpose for it. You might not know what it is today, or even tomorrow, but someday you will know and it will all make sense. Believe.

This book not only helps the victims of domestic violence but also provides a ray of hope to all those individuals faced with challenging tasks. It also boosts the necessary courage and willpower to accomplish all you want to achieve. You will learn to assert yourself and to walk, unshaken, toward the realization of your dreams of freedom.

Melissa January

Advice from the Author

Q. Were you afraid to leave?

A. I was very afraid to leave. Every time the thought of leaving would come up in my mind I thought that it was impossible because of my son I could never leave him. I had no identification, no finances, nowhere to go. I didn't feel secure in branching out on my own. I didn't feel that I'd be safe if I left. I was afraid of him coming after me, stalking me.

Q. When did you know it was time to leave?

A. After the last big fight I knew it was time to leave I feared for my life. I knew that I had a support system. Even though they didn't live close by, they were close enough. I knew that there was more ‘woman’ left in me and that I had the strength deep within to do something about my circumstances. Lastly, my love for God was restored. I knew he hadn’t given up on me just yet even though I had given up on him. There were many times when I could have died…when I should have died, but he didn’t let me. He never gave up on me. God says, “I will never leave you nor forsake you. I feel every bit of that now and can honestly say that he speaks the truth. I’m a living testimony.

Q. How did you feel when you finally left?

A. When I first left my abuser I felt empty and lost. I felt like I would never be able to love another person. I felt like I wasn't going to make it financially. I was so sure that I had made a decision of going back. In my mind I told myself that I was selfish because now my son would have to grow up without a father in his life. I was broken. After the first couple of days I began to feel relieved but then I started to miss him…not the man that abused me and nearly killed me. I missed the person who I had first fallen in love with. I missed the person who showered me with gifts daily. I missed the man that I shared vows with, the man that I thought I'd live with for the rest of my life.

Q. When did you know for certain that you would never go back?

A. I knew that I could never go back when I found out that he gotten engaged to another woman while I was on life support. The woman was pregnant by him as well but lost the baby. He had me and my son on a $50.00 a month spending limit while he was buying engagement rings for his other woman. That would have been the second child outside of our marriage.

Q. Despite all of it, did you ever consider going back?

A. I considered going back often. As a matter of-fact I went back once, only to find out that my abuser was still the same. I learned that he would never change. I was very insecure; I thought that no one else would want to be with me. Even though it was very dangerous being around him, I loved my husband and deep down I wanted to make our marriage work. I know it's hard to understand. I'm still lost about that fact too.

Q. How did it feel once you were free?

A. I wouldn't call it free... I don't feel free to this day... Freedom to me is different from where I've been or where I am, but I can definitely say it felt great when I got delivered. When I could go to bed and didn't have to worry about a drunken man coming home and waking me up demanding sex while I am sleep, then I feel free. I no longer have to hide my bruises and scars behind big shades. I can walk to the store and buy my favorite candy without holding my head down in shame.

Q. Were you afraid of what others would think?

A. Of course! I felt totally embarrassed. I thought that either people would feel sorry for me because of what happened to me or they would judge me and ask why did I stay. I especially assumed that others would question why I had allowed my son to go through all of this. If it was up to me I never would have shared my experience. It wasn't until the end of 2014 when I experienced my first form of healing. God started to shift my atmosphere. He changed my friends and my associates. He connected me with women that had been through what I' have been through. These women made me feel empowered. I then knew that I wasn't by myself anymore. I realized that I am a survivor; I am no longer a victim. I can now share my story in order to empower others who either went through the same thing or are currently going through the same thing. I have found myself throughout this journey. In turn, I have also found my purpose.

Q. Do you feel like you can ever trust a man again?

A. To be honest, yes I can. I can trust anyone until they give me a reason not to. I simply fly now... **First Love Yourself**. Meaning, I no longer put too much into who a person appears to be on the outside because clearly you are only meeting the representative in the beginning. I focus on knowing and loving me and what I'm meant to see within another person will be shown to me by God. I trust God completely and I hope he will give me the faith to trust everything else that is purposed for my good.

Q. Do you feel you can ever believe in love again?

A. I feel like I have a new appreciation for love. I totally trust love and I feel like whatever you put in you're going to get back. The more love you spread the more love you'll get back. I love differently now, but the most important love that I have found through this journey is the love for myself. To some it might sound selfish but I thank God that I now love myself. Make love not war. Love yourself first.

Q. How do you feel knowing that your child has seen you being abused?

A. That's a hard question to answer. I feel very bad to this day that I didn't just put myself through this, but I also put my son through it. My son is a survivor as well. I honor him daily. He has been through a lot at a young age and I just thank God for blessing me with him. I owe my son everything, that's why I work so hard now. He deserves the world.

Q. Did you share your story with your family?

A. Yes and No. I shared some of it but never really went in depth about the abuse. I never shared about the pill overdose either. I felt like they would judge me and tell me that I should have known they would always have my back. I felt that they would freak out knowing what he had done to me and my son and even worse that I still went back to him when I initially had the chance to free myself from the situation. They're never going to understand how their tomboy little sister got punked by her ex-husband. It seems like I always shared tough love so for them to know that I had fallen into a weak point in my life surely makes them feel some kind of way. If anything I hope they see that I'm human and that I too have a sensitive spot…knowing that I can be vulnerable and not always hard, but may make it easier for us to connect now.

National Domestic Violence Hotline 1-800-799-SAFE (7233) or 1-800-787-3224 (TTY)

59899332R00205

Made in the USA
Charleston, SC
17 August 2016